To hustle, to be considerate, t
to have initiative, to follow th
to cry, to hug, to inspire, **to help others**, to be loyal, to be
truthful, to be a winner, **to have fear,** to do the right thing, to
show up, to reach out to someone, to be clean, to be a leader,
to have passion, **to call a customer back,** to have respect, to
encourage, to make the right choices, to be kind, to commit to
excellence, to keep the faith, to take action, **to say no**, to make
a difference, **to make a commitment**, to shift your thoughts,
to be humble, to be reliable, to pray, to exercise, to take positive
actions, to be willing, to contribute in some way, to solve, to
measure, **to ask for directions,** to accept, **to recognize your
potential**, to understand, to be aware …

Eight Solutions that will Unlock Your Abilities

YOU DON'T NEED TALENT TO SUCCEED
BUT EVERYTHING ELSE COUNTS

Hector R. Hernandez

Foreword by Tim Corbin

iUniverse, Inc.
New York   Bloomington

You Don't Need Talent to Succeed
But Everything Else Counts

iUniverse books may be ordered through booksellers or by contacting:

iUniverse
1663 Liberty Drive
Bloomington, IN 47403
www.iuniverse.com
1-800-Authors (1-800-288-4677)

Because of the dynamic nature of the Internet, any Web addresses or
links contained in this book may have changed since publication and
may no longer be valid. The views expressed in this work are solely those
of the author and do not necessarily reflect the views of the publisher,
and the publisher hereby disclaims any responsibility for them.

ISBN: 978-1-4502-3425-2 (sc)
ISBN: 978-1-4502-3426-9 (dj)
ISBN: 978-1-4502-3427-6 (ebook)

Library of Congress Control Number: 2010907570

Printed in the United States of America

iUniverse rev. date: 06/25/2010

DEDICATION

To my family who have always been there for me in good and difficult times. You were the ones who helped me unlock my abilities. My love and gratitude for you is infinite.

TABLE OF CONTENTS

FOREWORD

My first thought in agreeing to write a foreword for Hector's book was, *Will my words do justice to the content of the book as well as to the trust that my writer friend has placed in me?*

I often think that God strategically places people in your life at various time periods—you have the choice of welcoming those people into your life or casually dismissing them. As a coach in college athletics, I have had the opportunity to establish relationships with many athletes—many of those relationships are long lasting even after their eligibility has expired. Very rarely does a parent of one of those athletes stay in my life … this is what makes Hector Hernandez different. I thought that Hector could have written a manual for "parent-coach relationships" because no one did it better than he. His respect was timeless—everyone called me Corbs, Coach, or Tim. Not Hector … he addressed me as Coach Corbin, and he does even today. He was selfless to the core, rooting on the team and everyone else's child as if he were his own. When he would come to the ballpark, he would run over to me like Secretariat crossing the finish line, with a huge smile on his face. "How are you? Great to see you!" he'd say. No one was immune from Hector's gregarious personality—coaches, players, parents, fans, stadium employees—everyone knew him. He was the ultimate energy giver every single day. If he wasn't there—which wasn't often—something was missing … he was an electrical charge that wasn't connected to a battery. Very few human beings have this effect on other people, an effect that can create a positive environment around them the way Hector could. Our personal relationship has remained close even since his son graduated from Vanderbilt. He is now my friend and, whether he knows it or not, he is a mentor to me.

"You don't need talent to succeed, Coach Corbin—you do

understand that, don't you?" Hector knew I would want to hear those words ... he could sense that I was listening and taking it all in, so he would give me more. He would tell me, "Everyone around you counts ... the laundry people, the groundskeepers, ticket takers, the public address announcer. How you handle those people is very important in the program's success. Your ability to inspire them and compliment them will make them feel as if they have a part in the team's success." Hector knew that I grasped that concept ... he knew that I bought into that notion 100 percent—and I did. He knew that I spent every waking minute thinking about the game of baseball, but he was actively "shifting my thinking" toward another aspect of program development that would encourage success. "You have everything you need to be successful, Coach Corbin ... now let it happen." I have thought about that statement manytimes, but not until I read his book did I start putting those thoughts together.

After his son's last game at Vanderbilt—in the NCAA baseball regionals in Atlanta—we walked out of the locker room after taking a shower. Before boarding the bus back to Nashville, the players were saying their "last good-byes" to their families. I was the last out of the locker room. As I glanced to my right, I saw a gentleman standing by himself in the darkness. As I got closer to him, I realized it was Hector. As I drew even closer to him, I could see tears streaming down his face. He reached out to me and said, "Thank you, Coach Corbin. I love you." He said nothing else. I will never forget his look or his words—they continue to inspire me daily

On the way home, all I could think about was Hector and how all his emotions had come to the surface on that June night. To most players, parents, and fans, the team's loss was the end of a season and an opportunity to go to the college world series. Hector felt this too, but so much more. To him, it was the end of many relationships that he had cultivated in two short years; he knew that he would always be part of the Vanderbilt family, but it would be different now.

I ask myself, "What is it about Hector that connects me to him?" It's his unyielding passion for other people, his everyday energy, his body language, his "will" and his "care" for other people. He celebrates every moment as if that day were his last—he absorbs every experience. He connects with every person that he meets because he sincerely wants to learn from them. A person's title, stature, or color doesn't matter to Hector. He is just building relationships and expanding his knowledge.

This book is him—it's Hector's personality ... every day ... every second of the day. He writes it. But, more importantly, he lives it. What makes him so unique is his inner ability to share his knowledge simply, with enthusiasm, and with respect to the reader.

I was fortunate to welcome Hector Hernandez and his guidance into my life! As I read Hector's book, I selfishly thought that he wrote it for me ... he actually wrote this book for you. Now read it, visualize it, and act upon your higher self.

Tim Corbin
Vanderbilt University

ACKNOWLEDGMENTS

I would like to express my love and gratitude to the following people:

To my wife Paula for always keeping me honest and being a great partner in my life.

To my children Brian and Jessica for teaching me what life is about through parenting.

To my parents Jose and Nerilda, who brought me and my brothers Luis and Tony "Cutin" to this great country to learn and prosper.

To my brothers Luis and Tony, whom I care for very much.

To my family on both sides who gave me love and accepted me for who I am.

To all my friends whom I grew up with and who have been there for me and my family for the past thirty-five years. Their support means the world to me.

To my teachers who had to put up with me through my early years and later in college, I am grateful.

To all my managers and mentors at IBM who gave me lessons in humility and leadership. I will not forget how much I learned from a great company like IBM.

To my friend Tim Corbin for taking the time to write the foreword. Coach, we appreciate the positive impact you made on our son Brian, my family, and all the other young men you have coached. I believe you have been applying "everything else." My family and I appreciate it.

To Marilyn Pincus, who listened to me and provided guidance, professionalism, and the nurturing of this book.

To all my friends at Dunkin' Donuts who inspire me every day.

To the United States of America for giving me and my family a foundation, opportunities, and the awareness that the ability we need to succeed is already inside of us.

About The Author

This is my first book. I have some questions.

First question: How should I introduce myself to you? Should I tell you I'm an inventor? Should I tell you I'm a professional speaker? I am a professional speaker with hundreds of formal presentations to major corporations, universities, and organizations, as well as K-12 public and private schools. Should I tell you I have worked for one company for the last thirty years, and this company paid for me to go to school to earn an undergraduate and a graduate degree? I did and they did. Should I tell you I'm a husband and a father? My wife Paula and I have been married more than thirty-one years. It's true.

Ah … but what is the most important thing to tell you here and now? I am 100 percent committed to a simple but brilliant approach to leading a successful life. I follow this approach and my cup runneth over. Once I realized *You Don't Need Talent to Succeed, But Everything Else Counts*, I was on my way. No matter where you start out in life, you can use the same simple but powerful approach I use and make your dreams come true. And, if your dreams are collecting dust, it's time to bring them out of the shadows and make them a part of your life!

Eight Years Old

I was eight years old when my family left Cuba. *Left Cuba* … two little words, eight little letters. The phrase doesn't begin to hint at the enormity of the event.

Several times, our journey had been about to begin when the "Do Not Pass" barrier was thrust across our paths. Once we were yanked back from the gates because the family name was incorrectly spelled (Fernandez instead of Hernandez!). Another time, the government wanted to see documents related to the sale of a car. My father had sold that car ten years earlier! The communist regime repeatedly played a cat-and-mouse game with the five of us—*now you're free to leave ... now you're not.*

My brothers were young and easily distracted from grown-up affairs. I was young too, but I vividly remember this time in my life.

I don't take America and my American citizenship for granted! When I look back over the last thirty years of work in corporate America, I'm enormously grateful for all my opportunities and experiences. Nothing has come my way because I was born with a silver spoon in my mouth. I wasn't!

Time and Time Again

After applying seven times before being hired and making my entry-level debut at International Business Machines (IBM), I progressed through a series of jobs that paid hourly wages: manufacturing, tape librarian, computer operator, software developer, management, education, project leader and sales. I've traveled to twenty countries to represent IBM, and I have met people from all walks of life. I have carried information to people within and without the company and—all the time—I was learning from them.

I have had the privilege of teaching at the university level as well as receiving numerous awards related to servicing others. I received my BA at thirty-one and my MBA at fifty-one years old.

I'm thoroughly convinced that everyone matters; everyone and everything counts.

I'm equally convinced that anyone who wants to know the joys of success can achieve success.

Ode to a Safety Pin

A safety pin is a small piece of metal, sharpened at one end, and bent back on itself to form a spring. There's a guard on the non-sharpened end that covers the point. The design is simple, and the result is brilliant!

The ancient Chinese philosopher Confucius (around 500 BCE) observed, "Life is really simple, but we insist on making it complicated." I know this to be true. I've always thought like this, and I take pleasure in sharing this truth with others.

I have designed this book for you. The concepts are simple. Use the words and messages as springs that can propel you forward into a bright future.

I hope with all my heart that you'll use this book as a guide to allow yourself to be better than you were in the past and to make a brilliant life for yourself.

I have no special talents. I am only passionately curious. It's not that I'm so smart, it's just that I stay with problems longer.

—Albert Einstein
Swiss-American physicist and
philosopher (1879–1955)

INTRODUCTION

Q: Do you realize you spend time each day with an amazing person?

That person is you!

Q: Do you know why you're amazing?

You came complete with an enormous number of abilities. When they were handed out, you were not permitted to say, "No thank you, I don't want any." Those abilities are pre-wired into your system.

Q: What does this mean?

It means you were born to succeed.

This book, *You Don't Need Talent To Succeed, But Everything Else Counts*, puts the spotlight on your abilities … my abilities … anyone's abilities. We all have the ability to be kind, strive for excellence, and keep commitments. We're able to be on time for appointments, willing to learn new things, and share. The list of our abilities is as long as a giraffe's neck, and realizing this isn't rocket science. Yet, the phenomenon of discovering that *you already have* what it takes to succeed is as potent as any fueled rocket at blastoff!

This book that you hold in your hands is like a safe that contains something precious. Imagine that it's secured with a combination lock. As you acquaint yourself with each chapter, you'll virtually be *turning the dial*. In no time at all, you'll crack the entire code and confidently map your journey to a successful future. *It doesn't get much better than that.*

The information in this book is written to help you unlock the abilities that are inside each and every one of us.

I provide passion, energy, and personal experiences with an exhilarating mission to help others succeed.

You'll feel at home with the content:

- easy-to-understand *delivery*
- easy-to-use *information*
- easy-to-remember *whys and wherefores*

Pay special attention to dynamic action descriptions. (They're about to be revealed to you.)

Words Guide our Actions

If I ask you to please turn right, you can turn right. You couldn't do it if you didn't know the meaning of the word *right*.

Watch yourself in slow motion and *see yourself think* before you act. You know what *right* means ... you turn right. It's easy.

Even if you have a great vocabulary and speak more than one language, you're about to find ways to use words that will take you on new adventures! I am a strong believer in the value of using words in the right way to change our lives. As an unknown author once wrote:

Watch your thoughts, they become words.

Watch your words, they become actions.

Watch your actions, they become your character.

Watch your character, it becomes your destiny.

It Happened to Me

Today, as I have for many years, I use the words *higher self* to refer to drawing upon my ability to *do something out of the ordinary ... rise to an occasion ... do something that was not expected.* This book contains illustrations to which all of us can relate.

I remember it as if it were yesterday ... I was having my usual morning coffee at my usual Dunkin' Donuts store when I overheard a conversation. What followed changed me forever!

An employee was telling the boss he would be coming to work late from now on. His bicycle had been stolen and he was going to walk to work. The boss didn't look too happy.

I was thinking about the man's misfortune when it occurred to me that I could get the man a bike. Before I went home that evening, I stopped at Wal-Mart and bought a bicycle. I brought it to him the next morning, and he was amazed. He couldn't understand why I had done this, but, when he realized the bike was his and there were no strings attached, he was overjoyed.

I felt fantastic, too.

At that moment, the words *higher self* hit me like a bolt of lightning. Every time I realized that *Hector can do better … Hector can make a positive difference*, I was connecting to my higher self.

After that experience, the words *higher self* started to guide my actions. Our thoughts "talk" to us and guide us. When we listen closely and shut out distractions, we know how to proceed.

All of us at some point have had the opportunity to do the *right thing*. A few years ago, for example, I was, once again, in Wal-Mart. As I was walking into the store, a middle-aged woman was talking on her cell phone. She stopped me to ask if I could help her with her car troubles. She was well dressed and groomed and had a frantic look on her face that suggested she was running out of options. She asked me if I spoke Spanish. I immediately told her I did not. I did this with a bad Spanish accent. I carried on with my business, selecting what I needed to buy. As I was shopping, a weird feeling came over me. I was feeling "lousy" about what I had said to the woman. I had misled her. I hurried my shopping with the intention of finding her and helping her. As I drove down every aisle of the parking lot looking for her, I was hoping she had not resolved her situation. At last I saw her. I approached her while calling to her in Spanish. I apologized about misleading her, and I told her I wanted to be of assistance. She was still very upset. Her car would not start, and her eighty-two-year-old mother was sitting in the backseat. The temperature was climbing. "I've got to get her to a cool place!" She also said there were six bags of groceries in the trunk that were sure to be spoiled. She had tried calling her husband, her brother, and a neighbor, but no one had responded. I told her not to worry, that I had battery jumper cables, and that I would help. I repeated how sorry I was for misleading her earlier. My knee-jerk response had been not to get involved. She told me we all make mistakes. "You are helping me now, and that is what counts the most."

Behavior is the mirror in which everyone shows their image.

—Johann Wolfgang von Goethe
German writer and philosopher

My higher self has been calling the shots for about ten years now. When I'm faced with serious challenges or special opportunities, I never go back to the beginning—to the way I operated before. These days, my higher self is my starting point! (I write more about this in chapter one.)

Since you don't need talent, and you already have everything else, you're about to discover how to unlock your success. You may not want a Mercedes in your garage, but you want something. Your dreams may include earning a college degree, making more money, moving a personal relationship to the next level, becoming a professional athlete, winning a world series at any level, adopting a child, or rekindling a relationship with a family member.

While writing this book, I was teaching a night class at a local college. When I talked to the students about higher self, a young student called Keith revealed that all he wanted was to speak to his sister. They had not spoken to one another for five years yet they lived within miles of one another in the same town.

Soon afterward, I introduced the dynamic action words *thought processor* to the class. We discussed what it is … how we all have one … how we are in control of it. Almost immediately, everyone in that class was using his or her "newly discovered" *thought processor.* Thought processor is your brain in motion. Did you ever think that your thoughts are actions in rehearsal? See yourself accomplishing goals that make you happy. Chapter three is devoted entirely to thought processor.

That night in the classroom, we spoke again of higher self. Most of these dynamic actions complement one another.

Two weeks later, Keith came to class eager to tell me, "I called my sister. We're going to meet." Keith told me privately he always knew he could do this, but he hadn't acted until he started to think differently: *Keith can do better—Keith can make a positive difference.* Keith's story is a prime example of the simplicity of applying the elements of "everything else" and acting on our thoughts. (There's more about "everything else" just before chapter one.) It may have taken Keith five years to act, but being in the class triggered his thoughts to take action and connect to his higher self—the same higher self that is inside each and every one of us. Throughout the school year, Keith kept giving me updates on his relationship with his sister and how they both bought a house together and are now back being a family again. It just takes that one simple turn in our thought processor to allow us to realize the ability we have to move things in the right direction.

Get It and Take Care of It

I've had the opportunity to speak to people around the world, and, almost 100 percent of the time, audiences immediately "connect" with the thought processor concept. *They get it!*

It's important to remember that there are times when you need to reboot—you need to use that thought processor with renewed vigor and determination. It has the capacity to get you where you want to go or, as James Allen explained, "You are today where your thoughts have brought you; you will be tomorrow where your thoughts take you."

James Allen was a nineteenth-century Englishman who wrote the book *As a Man Thinketh*. Reportedly Allen borrowed the book's title from the Biblical verse, "As a man thinketh, in his heart, so is he."

Keith and hundreds of others who attend my presentations, seminars, classes, and workshops understand and use some interesting concepts to expand their opportunities to grab hold of success:

- higher self
- thought processor
- rehearsing victory
- shift thinking

And these are just for starters! This book is filled with simple words that help you to think ... to see things from new and different perspectives. And, this book "talks" to everybody: mothers, fathers, significant others, athletes, employees, employers, teachers, students, friends, children, coaches, and neighbors ... everyone is able to:

- Use these words to rapidly identify dynamic actions
- Act with confidence since they know the actions are tried and true
- Feel free to chase and manifest any desire
- Do what it takes to put your Mercedes (*your* wish, desire) into your garage!

My goal is to help activate the abilities that are inside each and every one of us. It doesn't matter where you come from or the circumstances in which you find yourself right now. It doesn't matter how tall or short you are, or how thin or thick, young or old. The abilities to reach a *higher self* and to activate your *thought processor* belong to you right this minute! And, that's not all. There are eight dynamic actions revealed in this book ... one in each chapter.

The ancient Chinese thinker and philosopher, Confucius, said, "I hear and I forget. I see and I remember. I do and I understand." Keith *did*! He called his sister.

We know Keith now has *thought processor* down cold! You can do the very same thing. You will be ready to *do* what you want by using your thought processor and learning how to take other dynamic actions by the time you've finished reading this book.

A Superlative Bonus!

As I share these realities with more and more people, an extraordinary abundance of good things come my way. I don't know precisely how it all works, but I do know that, when you apply the eight dynamic actions in this book, you start to unlock the abilities that have always been with you, and this is something I think is well worth sharing. I just know I feel compelled to keep on helping others, and that is why I wrote this book. Start applying what you discover on these pages, and the good things that come your way shall be extraordinarily abundant too. Your *thought processor* returns what you load into it. It doesn't care what you load. It just returns what you load.

A book can reach millions ... it's my firm desire to reach as many people as possible. I want everyone to *discover how to be the best he or she can be.* I want people to be good to others and to share their know-how with others.

By the way, I competed with well-educated, highly qualified people during my first career, and I can tell you, without hesitation, that I was able to get noticed or designated project leader simply because I have everything else going for me! So, my assertion that *You Don't Need Talent To Succeed, But Everything Else Counts* is grounded in heavy doses of reality. And what you take from this book can become your future.

Henry David Thoreau, American author and essayist (1817–1862), said, "How many a man has dated a new era in his life from the reading of a book!" I hope this is true for all the readers of this book.

***

WARNING
You must accept full responsibility for achieving everything you always wanted.
If you can think of a more pleasant warning than this one, someone ought to buy you dinner!
Are you smiling? Good.
And now, let's unlock your abilities.

TALENT—a definition you can use

Something you can do better than one or two other people.
(That's it. It's simple.)

And, it's exciting to discover that you don't even need talent to
succeed.
Check out the Everything Else Page (it's next!).
If you do most of these things (anyone can do them),
you tap into an unending abundance of success.
If this sounds good to you, sit back, relax, and read on!

The Everything Else Page

This is a short but important list of some of the many things we can do without having any special talents. It is my intention to remind you that *all* of these abilities are already inside of you.

You don't need talent:

To believe in something, to believe in God, to be curious, to say thank you, **to be on time**, to be a good teammate, **to appreciate**, to think, to be reasonable, to answer your cell phone, to call your friends, to call your kids, to follow up on e-mail, **to help a teammate**, to change your thoughts, to change your life, to manage your career and life, to get a mentor, to be a mentor, to talk to your manager, **to let it go**, to get over it, to be an innovator, to be excited, to say I love you, **to say I'm sorry**, to quit, to try, **to be polite**, **to succeed**, to be rich, to care, to sit on your butt, to read, to go beyond what you know how to do, to ask how, **to be respectful**, to negotiate, to communicate, to learn, **to contribute**, to solve problems, to lead, to have passion, to innovate, to be willing, **to stay ready**, to apply D-I-S-H (read on!), **to be early**, to be late, to understand, to stay healthy, to share, to create, to accomplish, to set goals, to plan, to feel for others, **to be kind**, to hustle, to be considerate, to give back, to educate yourself, to have initiative, to follow the law, **to get up early**, to smile, to cry, to hug, to inspire, **to help others**, to be loyal, to be truthful, to be a winner, **to have fear**, to do the right thing, to show up, to reach out to someone, to be clean, to be a leader, to have passion, **to call a customer back**, to have respect, to encourage, to make the right choices, to be kind, to commit to excellence, to keep the faith, to take action, **to say no**, to make a difference, **to make a commitment**, to shift your thoughts, to be humble, to be reliable, to pray, to exercise, to take positive actions, to be willing, to contribute in some way, to solve, to measure, **to ask for directions**, to accept, **to recognize your potential**, to understand, to be aware, to be alert, to do extra, to work overtime, to sell yourself, to write a resume, to have a good interview, **to prepare**, **to practice**, to go out of your way, to listen to a webcast, to think outside the box, to be a TSR (read on!), to listen, to apply for a job, to ask questions, **to say good morning**, to say, "Nice job," **to pick up your neighbor's garbage**, to make the bed, to read the newspaper, to have ideas, to have joy, to be disciplined, to change your mind, to stay in touch, to engage, to make money, **to stay out of trouble,** to social network, to exercise creativity, to never eat alone, to love the game, **to pay for lunch**, to start a blog, **to send a birthday card,** to write notes, to write a book, to be better than yesterday, to go back to school, to become a speaker, to enhance your language, **to stay an extra half hour**, to buy a bike, **to change your behavior**, to break habits, to associate with the right people, to watch the History Channel, to visualize, **to rehearse victory,** to prioritize, **to reach a higher self**, to be a little more organized, to hold the door, to buy the person behind you coffee, **to subscribe to free magazines**, to do something out of the ordinary, to get ten sales leads each day, to trust, to be stuck-on-stupid, **to focus longer**, to go for a walk, to listen to success CDs, to slow down, **to allow good things to happen to you**, to take a class at your local college, **to vote**, to sing, to play a sport, to buy a book, to forgive, **to fail**, to argue about stupid things, **to be a good example**, to avoid using foul language, to have a strategy, **to be a professional**, to volunteer, to have ambitions, to question why, to resist, to do nothing, **to be lazy** …

You can ...

Open the book to any chapter and start reading. No one topic is more important than the others. I start with "Reaching Your Higher Self" in chapter one.

CHAPTER ONE

The First Solution:
Reaching Your Higher Self

What you spend years creating, others could destroy overnight. Create anyway. The good you do today will often be forgotten. Do good anyway.

Reportedly, this advice is written on the walls of Mother Teresa's home for children in Calcutta, India. Many other "instructions" were displayed along with these two.

When you do out-of-the-ordinary things and obtain outstanding results, you're putting your *higher self* to work. (I discussed *higher self* in this book's introduction. If you bypassed this and started here, why not take a moment and read the introduction now.)

Every one of the chapters in this book is peppered with stories that spotlight ordinary people doing out-of-the-ordinary things and obtaining outstanding results. I invite you now, as you explore chapter one, to:

- Read the stories.

- Mimic, copy, *steal* ideas and actions you can use!

- Use what you can now.

- Come back again, anytime, to read and review.

Story: A grandma was recently mentioned in a local newspaper. It took her fifty-two years to earn her college degree. She always had the ability to attend classes, complete assignments, and satisfy all requirements for graduation, but she didn't do it. One day, she gave the whole thing a lot of thought and came up with the reason she "couldn't" do it: "I'm afraid. What will people say about a grandma in college? They'll think I'm a foolish woman and talk about me behind my back. They'll want to tell me to act my age. I'm not a strong person, and that will hurt me." She went on and on with all the reasons why she couldn't ... shouldn't ... didn't. One day, she realized she had courage. Everyone does. Courage was *already inside of her* and all she had to do was *open the spigot and let it flow*! We know she did because we know she earned her college degree. This college graduate used her noggin ... her head ... her *cabeza*! She was reaching higher, stepping away from *ordinary* thinking and operating with what I—and many others—call *higher self.*

As a child, I didn't think about higher self, but there were a few people in my "world" who were—knowingly or unknowingly—preparing me to find it. One was my Aunt Aña. Another was my dad's Uncle Raul. Of course, my mom and dad (Nerilda and Jose) influenced my young life too. They set high standards and were our partners and friends. (I still speak to my mom every day!)

When I was five or six years old, my parents didn't have their own home so we lived with my aunt and uncle in Havana. Aunt Aña was always teaching my two brothers and me something valuable. She put a heavy emphasis on respect and taught us good manners. All we had to do was to follow her lead. I remember a hundred little scenarios about that time of my life; one was me watching her facial expressions as we were leaving Cuba.

When we arrived in America, my dad's Uncle Raul received us. He sponsored us coming to this country and welcomed us to his home. He gave my parents his bedroom. He, too, did innumerable gracious things to make us feel comfortable and make sure we were on the right track as we settled into our new lives. I stay in touch with Raul and would do anything I could for him because I know what he did for us when we moved here. My aunt passed away, but I sense that she is with me daily. It's fair to say that my aunt and uncle operated at higher self. They were excellent role models. My family and I appreciated everything they did. I still do today.

Newspaper Delivery

Story: When I was eleven years old I said, "Yes" to a man in our neighborhood who was hiring boys to deliver newspapers. I didn't know what this meant. I didn't know you had to wake up at 5:00 AM. I was eleven years old and I wanted to make money. In a movie, I had seen a stack of money wrapped in a rubber band. I began to think about having my own stack of money and knew this man was offering me a job, and a job meant money. I needed my parents' permission and didn't think they would give it to me. I realized this was something I really wanted to do. I kept seeing myself sorting money and putting it into stacks. So, I convinced my older brothers to deliver papers with me, and my parents agreed to let us work together.

Now I know that I was *rehearsing victory* (see chapter two) when I "saw myself" sorting money and putting it into stacks. The prize could have been blue marbles and not money. I focused on the stack of dollars because—at age eleven—I thought that was *neat*.

I was reaching my higher self when I didn't settle for the ordinary. I knew my parents wouldn't give me permission. I asked myself, "Why can't you do it?" I knew that I could … I just had to find a realistic way to fulfill my desire.

I depended on my *thought processor* to lead me to the realization that my brothers could be enlisted to help me get the desired result … my parents' permission. (You have a *thought processor* too! See chapter three for details.)

Billboards on the Roadside

Story: When I was a child, my parents traveled to Miami every other Saturday to see family members—

my uncle and his family. We had lived in Miami when we left Cuba and arrived in America in 1966. While we were still there, my Dad got a job 200 miles away from Miami. After awhile, the commute became tiresome so my parents settled in West Palm Beach, Florida—just thirty-five or forty miles from Dad's work. So, every other Saturday, we "hit the road." On these trips, I began to think about my *abilities* when I discovered I was able to memorize the advertisements featured on every single billboard as we traveled north and every single billboard as we traveled south. "The next billboard is going to say ..." "The next one is going to say ..." I tested myself and discovered I was a winner! (Try this with your children. It's fantastic.)

Now I know that I was learning what it felt like to be successful! When I remembered the upcoming billboard before I saw it, I was victorious. I spent those trips celebrating victory ... one hour and one-half there and one hour and one-half back. I was a little kid but realized I could memorize, rehearse, realize a desire (to know what was advertised on the next billboard) and fulfill that desire. I had learned how to set a goal ... a very specific goal.

Today, when I appear in front of audiences, I'm able to say with conviction, "Plant your goal. Fix it in your thoughts." A common phrase heard in business circles is, "Nothing happens until somebody sells something!" If you're sold on what you want, something will happen!

Use the S-M-A-R-T Factor

S = Solver

You're a problem *solver.* You look for solutions. There are problems to be solved everywhere—in business, at home, at school, and in the community. Problem solvers are in demand! Your solution could be something as simple as taking out the trash bins for a neighbor because that neighbor must be at the airport at 6:00 AM. She doesn't want to take out those bins in the wee hours of the morning when it's dark and when noise is bound to disturb neighbors. She thinks of you. "Hector, would you please put our trash bins curbside in the morning?" Done! Problem solved.

M = Measure

Can you tell where you are today? I go back in my thoughts to a picture of a scoreboard and ask myself, *Where am I from a scoreboard perspective? Where was I?* When you measure progress, you sometimes "see" the reward. Other times, a reward won't show up for years and years. So, for purposes of measurement, forget about rewards. *Where was I then? Where am I now?* A simple habit of asking and answering these questions will tell you something about yourself. If you are passionate about fulfilling goals ... chasing desires ... you've got to get started! Keep moving forward even if progress is slow. *Where am I?* The answer tends to motivate us to keep moving to get to where we want to go.

A = Action

Are you *really* a problem solver? You don't have to wait until you earn an advanced degree, *you've already got what it takes*, and the fact is that you are solving problems all the time. Here's something to think about ... If a man steals a loaf of bread to solve the problem of feeding hungry children, he's setting himself up for trouble. If this same man borrows money to buy bread and feed the children, he must repay the loan, but he hasn't invited trouble. The children eat. The man may get a part-time job or sell his ring to raise money. He may enroll in a training program that will lead him to a job with higher wages. Actions can vary and results vary too. The smart person acts wisely. That person is "realistic."

R = Realistic

One student in the college classroom where I teach a

night class left his book home the night I was discussing the *smart factor* with the class. Another student said, "Hector, just for tonight why can't we make a copy of this chapter and give it to Jay? Next time, he'll have his book with him, but for tonight we've solved the problem." This was a realistic solution.

T = Thoughts

You must shift your thoughts to focus on what you want. Your thoughts are actions in rehearsal. So, if your thoughts are in the right place, you're going to take the right action. Norman Vincent Peale (American clergyman and author, 1898–1993) once said, "We are what we think about all day long." A friend told me she is going to the gym to lose weight. She asked me what I thought about exercise. "I think exercise is important, and that's what you do when you go to the gym. You exercise." Since she's a good friend, I was able to add, "If you think you're losing weight, your thoughts aren't in the right place. You may lose weight as a result of the exercise, but, when you go to the gym, you should focus entirely on the exercise. Otherwise, you may be inclined to sit in the lounge and chit-chat too long instead of being on the treadmill. In short, shift your thoughts so they align with your desire."

S-M-A-R-T can be broken down in many ways. I've just given you one perspective, but, at the end of the day, I like to say that S-M-A-R-T also means *sincere motivation and action required today/tomorrow.* If you want to stay ahead of the pack, try adding E-R, which gives you S-M-A-R-T-E-R. The *E* stands for *every day.* And the *R* stands for *reap the reward.*

Story: I was twenty-one years old and (finally, after seven attempts) hired by IBM as a computer operator. I thought everyone who worked there must be a genius. Well, there are intelligent people and there are people who don't fit that description! They happened to be hired because they had a particular degree, or an opportunity opened because the company was growing. They were in an environment where they could be successful, but that didn't mean success was automatic. I started by *smelling* the environment— showing up a little early to inhale what I could see ... what I could hear. I was sniffing around to pick up a scent!

I didn't have a degree. I had enrolled in a couple of junior college courses, and I started thinking, *The company has a tuition plan.* I starting asking other employees, "Hey, are you doing this thing called a tuition plan?" I got negative answers: "No." "I don't have time for that." "I have a job." I asked, "Well, are you taking advantage of some of the classes when our shift is over?" (We worked from midnight until nine in the morning.) Co-workers told me they were tired. "I've got to go home and sleep and get ready for the next night." I asked myself, W*hat if I ask for tuition and go back to school? The opportunity is there.* It's part of the environment. I was tuning in to *higher self* ... thinking of ways that *Hector could do better.* I eventually earned a bachelor's degree and a master's degree, and IBM paid my tuition.

When I started to work for IBM in 1980, I was earning $2.15 an hour. Before long, I was asking if there was something more I could do. I was doing my normal job with time to spare. The supervisor said, "Don't make others feel like they're slower. Don't do that." I agreed, but I needed more to do. He told me to read some books. "What books should I read?" He gave me the procedures manual to read, and it didn't take long to realize that a lot of answers to the questions we'd been struggling with on the night shift were in that manual. Nobody had read it. Well, I could read!

I asked this supervisor if I could make a copy of the manual. "Nobody makes a copy ... it's just a procedures manual!" After I got permission, I copied the first procedure. I took it home and I read it. I copied the next procedure. I read it. And so on—until I was very familiar with everything in that 130-page procedures manual.

One night, we walked into the office and there was a huge problem. Systems were down. I looked over someone's shoulder at his computer screen and noticed that lights were all red where they should be green. I stepped back. I didn't say anything. I'd only been working at IBM for about six months. I could be wrong. I didn't want to embarrass myself. Then, too, there could be a way for me to be a hero. Maybe I could get a promotion out of this. Clearly, I was operating at my *lower self*!

My manager walked over to me. "You know what's wrong, don't you?"

"Yeah. I think I know what's wrong."

He asked me to come into his office with him and he explained, "In this company, we share as much as we can. Holding things close to the vest will not get you what you want. This may work in other companies, but it doesn't work here. The more you share, the more you're going to have. I've been here for twenty-five years … I know what I'm talking about. Now, what's the problem?"

"It's controller 3725. You've got a bottleneck in this router."

"Let's go out there right now, and you can tell Ray what you just told me." (Ray was the supervisor.) Ray realized that what I told him made sense. He followed through, and we were back in business!

From that point on I shared with everybody!

As I write this book, I've been with IBM for thirty years. This experience probably influenced the kickoff to my exciting and rewarding career more than anything else. I'm forever indebted to that very astute manager who "saw" me hesitate and quickly guided me to do better—to reach my *higher self*!

A Mentor

> *My chief want in life is someone who shall make me do what I can.*
>
> — Ralph Waldo Emerson
> American essayist, philosopher, and poet

I've had many mentors. Everybody around you matters—everybody. Don't just pick certain people. I think it's a great idea to go to lunch with different people as much as possible. Introduce yourself to someone you don't yet know. In this way, you create a network that can transform you from the "as is Hector" to the "to be Hector."

I'm a guy who likes to get other people excited about life ... you know ... always sharing ideas about how to better yourself. So, I am a mentor. And, as I'm fond of saying ... you don't need talent *to attract a mentor or to be a mentor*, but everything else counts.

Story: I was at the airport in Cincinnati and running late. I had just passed through security and had about thirty-five minutes to catch my flight. But, as I was coming out of security, someone called to me, "Hey, man, you want your shoes shined?" I looked at my watch and thought, *I don't have enough time.* But then I kicked into my higher self. *This individual makes his living shining shoes,* I reminded myself. *I'm going to make time.* So I said, "Sure." I sat down in the chair and asked, "How are you doing today?"

"Today has been a great day. Jesus has been good to me."

"That's wonderful. How was yesterday?"

"Terrible. Not a good day. And ... hey, man, you want a $5.50 or you want a $6.50 spit shine?"

"What's the difference?"

"One is shinier than the other."

"You know what? Give me the $6.50 shine. So, yesterday was not so good?"

He nodded.

"Why don't you do this," I offered. "Why don't you charge everyone $5.50 today because today has been a good day? You can do it from this point on."

He looked at me and asked, "Who are you?"

"I'm just a guy who has got to get to his flight." We laughed.

"You know," I continued, "if you charge $5.50, people are probably going to give you a $2 tip. If you charge $6.50, they may only give you one dollar."

"Who are you?"

"Don't worry about that. I'll tell you in a minute. You know what else you should do?"

"What?"

"When potential customers come through security, instead of saying, 'Hey, man, do you want your shoes shined?' you could say, 'Sir, would you like your shoes serviced?'"

"Oh, that's a good one."

"And don't call it a spit shine. Say, 'Sir, would you like your shoes detailed?'"

"Who *are* you?"

"I'm Hector Hernandez."

We talked about me and my work for a minute, and then I asked, "What's the name of your business?"

"Shoe Shine."

"Call it Red Carpet Shoe Shine. Go to the store and buy yourself a little red carpet. When the next customer is coming toward you, say, 'I'd like to put the red carpet out for you.' And do it."

"Oh my gosh. Jesus has been good to me."

You probably won't be surprised by what I said next—"You need to shift a little. It doesn't take talent to do that. You have the ability inside of you to think this way. All you have to do is step back and say, 'What can I do better for myself, for my customers, for the airport?' Do something out of the ordinary and you'll see your life shifting."

The shoe-shine man was a high school dropout, but, when we parted, he was on his way to enjoying greater business success. He was advancing confidently toward a worthy ideal! People ask me if I ever checked back with this man. I haven't had a chance yet, but I've got to go to Ohio soon, and I think I'll go through Cincinnati.

Story: I'm blessed with lots of energy. My mom and dad could tell you all about it! I was all over the place with this energy until I matured and started to channel it toward helping others. Not too long ago, a friend of ours I hadn't seen in years visited his brother who was our neighbor. We all went to dinner together. Eventually I was asked, "What are you up to?" I explained that I was writing a book entitled: *You Don't Have To Have Talent To Succeed, But Everything Else Counts.* My friend was riveted to the words. "My son needs this."

I knew his son had conflict management issues and a long trail of difficulties behind him. "Dan keeps saying he doesn't have the talent it takes to be successful, and you're telling me it's all about everything else?" My friend went on to explain, "If Dan could just understand how simple 'everything else' is! He acts, but he doesn't do it with a focus … he doesn't do it with an attitude, he doesn't do it with a planned approach. His energy and actions are scattered all over the place! He doesn't do things in an orderly fashion."

I told the father, "Almost everyone has these thoughts—*I don't have talent … I don't have what it takes to be successful.* When I break it down during seminars or workshops—or in my book—people can see it from a place of safety. I tell the story from my point of view and people connect with me. 'That's me!' they say. 'I am sort of lost.' When I reach the middle of my presentation, I start putting things together with pictures, charts, visuals. Then people say, 'I get it. That is what I need to do.' The fact is, I'm not telling them anything new. I'm reshaping the information to make people aware. Everything I tell them keeps going back to one point—*it's inside of you!*"

Story: A young man was earning a good living as a pharmacy technician, but he hated his work. He enjoyed fixing things with his hands. He decided to become certified as an auto mechanic. "Are you crazy?" his friends asked when he told them what he was doing. "You're making good money now, and, besides, people really respect a pharmacy technician." Focusing on his desire to please others was the thing that had kept him depressed for thirteen years! When he attended auto mechanic classes, most of the other students weren't well spoken or well groomed. They never mentioned best-selling books or classical music, and they often talked about problems with the law and women. He was in an unfamiliar world, but he was happy. He asked himself, *Why didn't I do this a long time ago?* I recently read this quote by an unknown author: *Joy is a flower that blooms when you do.* I must mention it to this young man. He will understand.

Multiple Choice Challenges—For Your Eyes Only

1. Do you feel joyful or motivated to act when you watch others succeed?

   Always—Sometimes—Never

   - **Always?** Take a bow. Success is an attention grabber, especially when you're tuned into your higher self. No one will see your "score" unless you want to show it off, but ... go ahead ... in addition to taking a bow, award yourself *5 points*.

   - **Sometimes?** This suggests that your powers of observation need some exercise! "Some cause happiness wherever they go; others whenever they go," said Oscar Wilde (Irish writer, 1854–1900). Multiple opportunities to cause happiness are missed when you don't pay attention to *all* the "good stuff" around you. Send an e-mail or shake someone's hand to acknowledge his or her success. Go out there and find a shoe-shine guy. Your higher self is in high gear when you cause happiness. Award yourself *3 points* and promise yourself to do better.

- **Never?** Try tuning in to other people and their achievements. If you're willing to try, give yourself *2 points*. (By the way, your higher self just kicked in!)

2. Do you avoid certain people?
    Often—and with good reason!
    No—I don't admire such behavior.

- **Often?** Get ready to re-think this response. What are you missing? You probably can't answer this question because you weren't *there*! Sorry, you earn **0 points** for this response.

- **No?** You may decide not to spend much time with a person you would rather not see at all, but it's not productive to avoid that person altogether. Dame Julie Andrews (English film and stage actress, singer, and author, 1936–) said, "Perseverance is failing nineteen times and succeeding the twentieth." Doesn't it sound as though Miss Andrews was reaching for her higher self? Will your perseverance enable you to build a productive relationship with those you'd rather avoid? It's possible, and little is lost for the trying. You have just earned *5 points*!

This is one of three quizzes in this book. Keep track of your points earned in this quiz and add them to the next set.

Points earned this time _____ **(possible 10)**

CHAPTER TWO

—————— ❁ ——————

The Second Solution: Rehearsing Victory — Prepare, Practice, Prepare, Practice, and Just *Go with the Flow*

You can really have everything you want, if you go after it, but you will have to want it. The desire for success must be so strong within you that it is the very breath of your life / your first thought when you awaken in the morning, your last thought when you go to bed at night ...

Concentrate all your thoughts on the great desire in your life. This concentration must be continuous, unceasing every minute; every hour; every day; every week.

— Charles E. Popplestone
Twentieth-century motivational author

When you *see, feel, think, and smell success* before it arrives, you're ready to receive it. You're miles ahead of competitors who don't know *precisely* what to expect. When the time comes to act, you'll simply repeat your performance. You already know you're going to be victorious.

Every one of the chapters in this book is peppered with stories that spotlight ordinary people doing out-of-the-ordinary things and obtaining outstanding results. I invite you now, as you explore chapter two, to:

- Read the stories.
- Mimic, copy, *steal* ideas and actions you can use!
- Use what you can now.
- Come back again, anytime, to read and review.

If you ever wanted to give up on something (for example, your studies, your job) this is your story! The fact is, it's everyone's story. I hear it at least ten times a month. Here's a problem: The temptation to give up is at the highest level just when you are about to succeed.

It's what I tell people who attend my classes, workshops, and presentations. I probably picked up the words from Bob Parsons, a businessman I admire. If you look at Bob's www.godaddy.com Web site, he mentions that this is an old Chinese saying. No matter who said it first, it behooves you to remember it. And then get back to rehearsing victory.

Story: In chapter one, I mentioned "smelling the environment." This concept deserves discussion now too. When I worked the midnight-to-eight AM shift, during my breaks, I walked up and down corridors. I noticed that some people's offices were nicer than others. Some offices had curtains on the windows, others didn't. Some offices had handsome wooden desks, and others had Formica-top desks. Some office floors were covered in posh carpets, others were not. I was curious about who "belonged" in these offices. One day, when my shift ended, I waited around and kept an eye on the doorway of the best-appointed office. I wanted to know whose office it was, and I had lots of questions for that person. I could see without being seen. (Fact is, I was hiding behind a wall!) I had some fear about approaching that person so I didn't do it. But I decided to do the same thing in another building. One day, I "bumped into" a man as he was about to enter a large and beautiful office that I had noticed.

"I'm sorry. I was just out here admiring your office," I said to him.

"Come on in," he offered

"This is a beautiful office. Can you tell me how you achieved this?"

He asked me about my job with IBM. When I told him I was an operator on the third shift, he told me, "That's an important job. Without you, we wouldn't have our work ready for us when we arrived in the mornings." This made me feel so good—and I didn't even know the man's first name! I felt more confident, and realized it was okay for me to ask questions. *I can really achieve this,* I told myself. *I can have it.*

When I went home, I told my wife Paula, "It's fun to work at my job. But it's not just work. It's more than work." These baby steps enabled me to better understand where I was heading. I could literally see the curtains on my office windows and the framed artwork on the walls when I "pictured" myself moving forward at IBM.

I learned that not all employees had the desire (or the sincere motivation) to better themselves. There were people who kept promises and people who didn't; not everyone cared. I decided I was going to find where the gaps were and squeeze myself into them. I figured that, if I did this consistently, I would be recognized—I would stand out. This is advice I give today when I speak to young executives and other groups of people. You always want to be learning, contributing, solving, and leading. When you learn, you are able to contribute. If you contribute enough, you start to solve problems, and that makes you a leader. This cycle can be repeated for every assignment or job you get for the rest of your career.

Story: When I was in eighth grade, a teacher told me I wasn't going to amount to anything, and that I talked too much. I didn't believe her. Dale Carnegie (American writer and lecturer, 1888–1955) said, "Develop success from failures. Discouragement and failure are two of the surest stepping-stones to success." I didn't know of Mr. Carnegie when I was an eighth grader, but, when I *refused to see failure*, I was *developing success*. In a sense, this was a form of *rehearsing victory*! I did it over and over again—I still do it!

At about the same time, I earned a place on a baseball team. Strangely enough, I got on the team because I cried. For the next two years, I warmed the bench. I had the opportunity to listen, watch, and learn. I discovered the ability to "listen" through my eyes as well as my ears. I learned a great deal about the game, the equipment, the team, the field, the bleachers, the umpires, the coach, and myself. Every sinew of my being was poised to win when I finally moved from the bench to the playing field.

Many years later, I was often on the field when my son Brian, who played college and professional ball, walked onto the field. Fans in the bleachers screamed as Brian got ready to swing. I didn't hear them. I felt as though I was connected to Brian ... as though I was helping him. I was sending him positive energy. I know this sounds "off the wall," but other parents tell me they experienced the same thing. Some said it was prayer. Famed author and motivational speaker Earl Nightingale (1921–1989) tells us: "The key that unlocks energy is Desire. It's also the key to a long and interesting life. If we expect to create any drive, any real force within ourselves, we have to get excited." During those private, intense, and focused minutes, I saw Brian succeed. Moments later, everyone else saw him succeed too.

Story: As I write this book, I'm winding down a thirty-year career with IBM. You may be surprised when I tell you that, as soon as I complete my last day with this wonderful company, I will turn my back on the past and focus exclusively on the present and the future. All I will see is the windshield in front of me. It's *big!* It's nothing like the little rearview mirror. I'll be rehearsing victory! I *see* myself on stage in front of audiences delivering presentations, feeling the energy, and helping others to be better and happier people. I'll *see* my motivational and inspirational books being read by people all over the world in multiple languages. In order to stay fully engaged in my future success, I know I must devote all my energies to it. Someone asked me, "Won't this be difficult?" I answered, "No. Because I've already rehearsed it, and I know what it looks like." When you're passionate about what you want, you think of it as something in your future—a done deal! Rehearsing victory is another one of those abilities we all possess. No talent necessary.

Story: The 2008 Tampa Bay Ray's baseball team had a long way to go to make baseball history, and that's putting it mildly. "The resuscitation hasn't been easy. It was an eight-year slide from an ownership that took the public for granted," says Bob Andelman, author of *Stadium for Rent: Tampa Bay's Quest for Baseball*. Yet available tickets for the first two games sold out in fifteen minutes when Sternberg, the new owner, took the leadership position. Here's what he said: "We put in new lighting, a new sound system. We scrubbed down the stadium. People were asking me why we were doing all that when the team lost all the time. We were preparing for success."

Story: American athlete Bruce Jenner was an underdog at the 1976 Olympics in the decathlon competition. This event typically consists of ten events that are held on two days. On the first day, there's the 100-meter run, the long jump, the shot put, the high jump, and the 400-meter run.
  On the second day, there's the 110-meter hurdles event followed by the discus throw, the pole vault, the javelin throw, and the 1500-meter run. I understand

that the day before the competition, Jenner walked into the empty stadium and absorbed it all. He had an American flag with him, and he opened it and started to run around the stadium with it, visualizing that, when he won, he would take a similar victory lap. He "felt" what it was like to celebrate the United States of America. Then he went one step further. He moved to the section of the stadium where his parents would be sitting. He gave them (imaginary) hugs and high fives and "heard" all the people sitting near his parents giving him their congratulations. He was rehearsing victory! Bruce Jenner won a gold medal in the decathlon in the 1976 Olympic games. He set a new world record for the decathlon with 8,176 points!

Here's an observation: You're building *mental strength* when you're *rehearsing victory*. Mental strength comes under the heading "everything else" (see the list in the front of this book). Most people know that Tiger Woods is loaded with talent for the game of golf, but that isn't what makes him a winner over and over and over. A headline in *USA Today* reads, "Tiger's biggest club is his mental strength." The article goes on to say, "Woods can focus to the exclusion of all else under pressure, especially when a major championship is on the line." Bob May, another pro golfer, observes, "Tiger is the most mentally tough guy in sports, from race car drivers to football players to anyone." You too have this ability to focus. I continue to talk about athletes and others in chapter six. In chapter six I talk about Tiger flipping number one and number two and having his life turn upside down; these things happen when we have our egos telling us that "I" and "Me" are the only ones that count.

Word Wisdom

I'm sure you've noticed that I use the term "rehearsing victory." It's just like "visualization," so why doesn't Hector just say "visualization"? Because it's a word that has been used to death! If you happen to come upon articles and books about visualization, however, I suggest that you read them. Read from start to finish so you don't miss important information. Sometimes something that can help you isn't mentioned until the end of the article or chapter.

8763 Hours

You've got the time to rehearse victory. How does Hector know this? Because everyone gets 8763 hours a year. Even if you subtract seven hours for sleep each night, you've still got 6205 hours. Think of those you admire for their success—they weren't given more or less time than you ... even rich people don't get more, and poor people don't get less.

Leonardo da Vinci (Italian painter, sculptor, and scientist, 1452–1519) said, "Time stays long enough for anyone who will use it." When you think about it from a new perspective, you may be less likely to say, "I'm too busy!"

Exploratory Interview

You ask for a thirty-minute conversation with an area manager or leader about a job that might interest you. You want to know what they do every day. You gather information and, in the process, decision makers get to know you. You might decide that, out of ten exploratory interviews, you'd like to pursue three jobs. Talk to your manager about these three areas, or call those three people and notify them, "I'm ready to pursue an opportunity in your ____ [fill in the blank]." This strategy works best in a large company, but I spoke to some heating, ventilation, and air-conditioning students and some automotive students. And I gave them a field trip assignment. Most of the students were thinking about where they wanted to work after they earned certification. I told them, "Wear your school shirt with the HVAC or automotive insignia so when you walk into a place of business, it's easy for others to tell that you're getting your education." Many of these potential employers wouldn't typically talk to these students, but, because of the "field trip" modus operandi, they did. The students were prepared to ask and answer lots of questions. Ten students out of thirty who participated in this experiment are being considered for jobs.

Letter to Coach

I wrote this letter to Coach Tim Corbin to show my support and to confirm that the ultimate reward in college baseball is just around the corner. Thomas Troward (English author, 1847–1916) wrote: If we could just "contemplate ourselves surrounded by the conditions we want to produce," we would be almost there.

> *May 10, 2008*
> *Coach Corbin,*
>   *Believe it or not, I am always thinking about our two years at Vanderbilt and the ten years we have known each other. When you respond to my e-mails, it connects me to you and Vandy baseball, and, for me, that is awesome.*
>   *I have many theories, and one that I am fond of is that nothing happens unless something moves. Our thoughts are the first movement in most of what we do, so I am a big believer in that our "thoughts are actions in rehearsal." That's where "rehearsing victory" comes from.*
>   *What's in this envelope is "simple" but it's what I know you, the team, fans, friends, administration, city of Nashville, university, and your family are seeking. Everything you want for you and your team is on its way, it will arrive precisely on God's timetable. Whatever you and your team experience that seems like a problem is temporary. What you desire is on its way and it's coming to you in amounts even greater than you can imagine. You need to hold on to these thoughts in a state of gratitude, no matter what.*
>   *What's in the envelope is a symbol of what you and others want. It's something that you will be asked about as new recruits tour your facility, and it should go right next to all of the other recognition awards.*
>   *To avoid any confusion, open it in two weeks or when you are ready, but after the season has ended no matter the outcome.*

You may find it strange that I would be sending something like this to you, but trust me when I say I mean no disrespect. On the contrary, this is something I know you think about and will have very soon, and I just wanted to provide a place for it. It's what I call rehearsing victory.

Thanks for your friendship and all you do for everyone.

Your friend,
Hector

CHAPTER THREE

The Third Solution:
Feeding Your Thought Processor

You are today where your thoughts have brought you;
you will be tomorrow where your thoughts take you.

—James Allen
British philosopher and writer

There is nothing entirely within our power but our own thoughts.

—Rene Descartes
French philosopher

It's a funny thing about life; if you refuse to accept anything
but the best, you very often get it.

—W. Somerset Maugham
English author

Change your thoughts and you change your world.

—Norman Vincent Peale
American clergyman and author

For thirty years, technology has played a major role in my work life. The word *processor* is an old, familiar one to me—it's another name for CPU, or *central processing unit*. And the CPU—or the processor—is the brain of a computer.

When your mental activity—your thinking ability—is finely

23

honed and you're able to make decisions that lead to actions that make you happy, you're in an enviable position! Use your *thought processor* (in other words, your mental activity ... your thinking ability) to bring happiness to others too. Although your aim is to give and not to receive, you shall be repaid a thousandfold.

Every one of the chapters in this book is peppered with stories that spotlight ordinary people doing out-of-the-ordinary things and obtaining outstanding results. I invite you now, as you explore chapter three, to:

- Read the stories.
- Mimic, copy, *steal* ideas and actions you can use!
- Use what you can now.
- Come back again, anytime, to read and review.

Standard Equipment

Your thought processor is pre-loaded. It's made when you're made! You have to activate it—boot it up—before it starts working. You must input information, then calculate and plan. Remember ... your computer/thought processor is a means to an end. Act on information you process. Make good things happen!

> **Story**: My brother Luis is outstanding at painting what is known as realistic cubism. (In this type of painting, the viewer is able to see the artist's objects from many different angles and points of view all at once.) Luis paints lots of ships and boats. For twenty years or so, he has earned his living working in a grocery store. I'm very proud of my brother's abilities, and, over the years, I have frequently urged him to paint for others and sell his work. As I write this book, Luis is painting two large paintings for prospective customers.
>
> How did this happen? Luis knows about my seminars, workshops, and presentations. We talk about how "everything else counts," and, at some point, he put his thought processor to work to determine how to do more with his paintings. When I read about a

Latin American art festival in West Palm Beach and mentioned it to Luis, he was ready to act. I was thrilled when he asked me to help by writing the abstracts he needed to accompany his entries. There weren't any awards offered at this show, but lots of people came to see it, and they saw his work. He made a lot of connections.

It all began with *activating* "everything else specifics." When that happened, Luis's thought processor began to work differently from the way it had for the last twenty years. And Luis is doing things he has never done before. I'm bursting-my-buttons proud of my brother's achievements, and it's a joy to see him so happy about this new turn in his road.

Story: This story is about my mom, Nerilda. (Let me jump back for a moment and remind you, as I mentioned earlier, that many topics, ideas, and thoughts overlap in this book. Thought processor isn't strictly confined to this chapter, for example, and rehearsing victory isn't strictly confined to chapter two. And so it goes.)

My mother has always had an amazing thought processor. One of the things she used it for when we were kids was to make sure we took care of "everything else." My mother is a self-taught office manager who worked in a huge department store in Cuba. When we came to America, she didn't try to pursue that career. Instead, she got a job in a factory. She left for work very early in the morning, and she left little reminders for my young brothers and me. In those years we didn't have those ready-made Post-it® notes, but my mom wrote her messages and posted them all over the house with Scotch® tape. "Don't forget to turn off the oven." "Don't forget to lock the front door." She was communicating with us all the time even when she couldn't be with us! She wanted us to remember we had responsibilities. (Part of "everything else" is doing all the little things you should do such as return telephone calls promptly, send a card to someone who is celebrating a birthday or an anniversary, route a pertinent article to a colleague when you believe it will be of interest to him, visit someone who is hospitalized, send flowers on special occasions.) I suspect I'm the *attentive* person I am today, in part, because of the foundation my mother laid for us.

Whatever my mom tackles, she tackles with zeal. One of her callings on this planet is taking care of animals. She's known as the Cat Lady. Every cat in the neighborhood finds its way to my parents' house. People donate money to Mom to use for the strays. She sees to it they are spayed or neutered, and she makes sure they are fed and loved, thus reaching her own personal higher self.

No matter whether you're earning a living as an office manager or a factory worker, raising a family of rambunctious boys or caring for homeless cats, your thought processor calls the shots and you act accordingly! It helps when you have parents who are excellent role models.

Story: I put the following "desire" into my thought processor fifteen years ago: someday I want to teach young adults in an academic setting. As soon as I graduated with my MBA, I came across the help wanted information in the newspaper. I knew the time to act had come. I'm currently teaching leadership classes at a local college.

I try to make all my presentations, lectures, and seminars entertaining. I always get smiles when I announce, "This is a BYOT gathering." Bring your own thoughts.

Story: I met a man on an airplane who earned his living repairing cast iron ovens. He is one of less than a handful of people who do this work; he travels all over the world to serve customers. When he told me he was on his way to Italy, I did a double take.

"You've got to be kidding me! You're going all the way to Italy to fix an oven?"

"I've got a little shop in Louisiana. I employ ten toolmakers who can make and supply parts I need and send them to me via overnight mail. I've got to examine an oven before I know what tools and parts are required. I've got some basic items with me, but typically some customized parts are required." He went on to explain that these are huge ovens that are handed down from generation to generation.

"Do you know the problem you're going to fix?" I asked him.

"Not really. I know the symptoms, but I don't know what is happening."

"Wow. That is an incredible job!"

He asked me what I did for a living, and, before you know it, we were speaking with one another as though we were old friends.

I asked a delicate question, "Do you believe the ovens at some point start talking to you? Or can you somehow relate to these ovens?"

And without hesitation he said, "Absolutely!" And then he added, "I wake up at two or three o'clock in the morning and start thinking about my ovens."

I told him, "Man, you're now in my world. Physical things have energy. Physical things have feelings."

"I'm afraid to tell people that I talk to the ovens and they talk back to me. I feel like a doctor ... I feel as though the ovens know they're going to survive."

Then I had a thought. I said, "I'm going to find a spot for what you're telling me when I make presentations."

"No way!" he said, really getting excited.

"Absolutely—because it deals with everything I believe in."

Tears appeared in his eyes, and I asked if something was wrong.

"No," he said. "I want you to spread the word. I want you to tell the story because these ovens need representation."

I think of him now because he uses his thought processor to "connect" to his ovens. When he spoke to me of his work, he was passionate. His eyes glowed with happiness, and his very large body visibly relaxed in the small airplane seat he occupied next to me. He's in his work environment almost daily and knows he's going to be able to repair a particular oven because he's in a special state of mind ... a state of gratitude every time he is sent off to work his magic. He "feels" the oven connecting to him ... *I am willing to accept you. I am willing to let you help me.* Even though the oven is an inanimate object, this man explained there is a connection. As a result, he knows he is very much in touch with his "source" ... a greater power. He is not alone. He is aware that the more he provides—the more good he does—the more he receives back. He said, "*Abundant good* bounces back to me!" Needless to say, this airplane trip went very quickly for me. This man was telling me what I tell seminar and workshop attendees. Help somebody—or something—and you really help yourself. It begins when you feed that notion to your thought processor. It may take months or years of operating this way, but eventually you reach a point when you *know* this works. Nothing can get in the way. At that point your confidence reaches a new level. (Does this take talent? Absolutely *not.*)

Before this delightful human being took the seat next to me, I had watched him walking down the aisle toward me. My immediate thought had been, *I hope this isn't the person who is going to sit next to me.* By now I should know better. He is about 6'5", weighs about 300 pounds, and, on that day, he looked exhausted. I even surmised he would have a body odor. If I hadn't quickly reached for my higher self, I would have told him the seat wasn't available—and I would have missed the conversation of a lifetime! Whenever I can, I do talk about him and his ovens and his passion. Not everyone is ready to accept what he and I spoke about … people cut me off and don't believe me, but there's a percentage of people in every audience I address who relate to this. They may not want to admit it, but there are "inanimate" objects in their lives that parallel this man's ovens, and they know precisely what this man experiences. We all need to find the oven in our life. This is a good time to mention Michael Jordan's words … "You have to expect things of yourself before you can do them." (Michael Jordan is a former NBA basketball player, born 1963).

> **Story**: There are times when you can overheat your thought processor. I'll give you an example. In 2007, the New England Patriots had a desire from the beginning of the season to win the Super Bowl. Every year, all thirty-two teams want to win the Super Bowl. Well, the New England Patriots had a remarkable record—they won eighteen games in a row! They were the first professional team since 1884 in any of the four major American sports (football, basketball, baseball, and hockey) to win the first eighteen games of their season. So, they arrived at the stadium for the Super Bowl with one desire … win one more little game. Three hours to go, and all they had to do was everything they'd been doing. *In three hours we're going to win the trophy!* They had the experienced players, great defense, awesome offense, and Tom Brady. Do you recall what happened? The New England Patriots *lost* that Super Bowl.

This team had talent, but, when it came to the Super Bowl game, *they weren't doing "everything else"* … something was different. Sports analysts have offered their opinions on the whys and wherefores … I offer mine here:

- Somehow, for some reason, the team members just allowed themselves to become disconnected from what they'd been connected to.

- Perhaps they started saying to themselves, "If we don't do this, we'll be so embarrassed."

- Or they might have said, "If we don't do this, we'll disappoint our fans, our families, the ownership … we'll disappoint all the team members."

All of the above statements—thoughts—are negative. They can creep right in if you aren't diligent! We have to keep these sorts of thoughts out of our minds. It's important to *allow* things to happen for us. In the case of the Patriots, they had the right team, they had the right organization … this pattern of thinking could have put them back on a positive track … success would have been just down the road! When you win eighteen games and are prepared, the rest should already be yours—this team deserved it.

The same goes for an interview, a job, a relationship, finances, and gaining other material things. The power to allow good things to happen to you and the knowledge that you have the abilities to do all the things you want to do are already part of you—these come with the package. John Wooden, the famous UCLA basketball coach (born 1910), once said, "Ability is a poor man's wealth." Let me conclude this chapter with this—Change or shift your thoughts in a positive manner, and you will change your feelings. Change your feelings, and you will change your behavior. Change your behavior, and you will change your outcomes, thus manifesting everything you always wanted. You have the ability to perform any of these tasks without any special talents.

CHAPTER FOUR

The Fourth Solution: Shifting Your Thinking

[Success] is the result of some good fortune to allow you to be in the right place at the right time, along with a willingness to work hard and make sacrifices; combined with the intelligence to know how and when to make adjustments; but mostly the drive to persevere regardless of any obstacles.

—Cal Ripken, Jr.
American professional athlete

If you correct your mind, the rest of your life will fall into place.

—Lao-Tzu
Chinese philosopher (traditionally sixth century BCE)

This paradigm for changing thinking that is ingrained by habit is all about helping you to change your thoughts. Enjoy this experience as you watch everything else just fall into place.

When you discover you can *switch-hit*, you'll be amazed by how you expand your horizons … add value to life. You may get stuck, but you won't stay stuck! According to ehow.com, a Web site that claims to have information on "How To Do Just About Everything," "Learning to switch-hit in baseball will increase your value to any team. The keys to switch-hitting are discipline, honed reflexes and repeated practice."

This sounds a lot like shifting our thinking. As Cal Ripken tells us, "Know how and when to make adjustments … persevere."

Please see the slices of Swiss cheese graphic at the end of this chapter. I've used this graphic in my presentations for a long time, and it gets so much positive feedback. "If I move the slices around just a little, I can see where one opening aligns with the next," said one seminar attendee. That, of course, is the point … shift your thinking and desires that were out of alignment … puzzling you … frustrating you … become easy to achieve! When new slices of cheese (goals) are added, they align with others and there's nothing blocking you. You continue moving forward.

Every one of the chapters in this book is peppered with stories that spotlight ordinary people doing out-of-the-ordinary things and obtaining outstanding results. I invite you now, as you explore chapter four, to:

- Read the stories.
- Mimic, copy, *steal* ideas and actions you can use!
- Use what you can now.
- Come back again, anytime, to read and review.

Story: I was about twenty-four years old and didn't have formal training in managing people. When Clancy Boswell, a well-respected IBM executive, approached me with a job opportunity, I declined! I thought, *I'm not ready for this. I don't have any education.* But the man wouldn't take "no" for an answer. He simply said, "You're the right person for the job."

I went to work. About six weeks later, I was asked to select two employees and recommend them for promotion. I did my homework and chose two people I knew were well qualified. When I submitted their names to the promotion board, they were immediately bumped down on the list … from position numbers ten and eleven to numbers thirty and thirty-one.

"Why is this happening to me?" I became emotional and expressed my lack of understanding to Clancy.

He laughed. "Hector, you're just hitting a wall. This is just a temporary thing. If you can't climb the wall, you go around it, even if it's a long wall. Since you're going to stay in management, you're going to have to be able to deal with issues, and your people are going to get promoted. I'm going to show you how it's done inside the IBM corporation, and I'm going to show you how to play the game. I'm going to show you the politics of all this!"

He gave me a tremendous boost on that day. I sincerely believed I could move and progress in a corporate management environment. Obviously, I shifted my thinking from *I can't* to *I can*. It wasn't a matter of snapping my fingers and making everything work … it took time and commitment. But once my thinking shifted, I was on my way.

If we did all the things we are capable of, we would literally astound ourselves.

—Thomas Alva Edison
American scientist and inventor

Story: I was once asked a question: Is it fair to assume that people coming out of college are filled with enthusiasm and want to do a great job and want to go places?

Here's my response: People typically fill out an application, submit it to the company, and wait for a response. If no response is forthcoming, they apply elsewhere. They may update their resumes and check the Internet, but they don't do some of the extra things you have to do (the "everything else") to continue to expand and create their network, but more important trigger and shift their thoughts to continual action.

Think how different my answer would have been if everyone were inclined to shift thinking!

Volunteering is a lost art, but it is a great way to be considered for a job. For example, say you approach the gas station owner in your neighborhood and make him an offer: "I can work for you on Thursdays without cost to you so I can learn how to do things such as fix the pumps and work a register." Now, this is an offer that's hard to refuse. Admittedly, some people will turn you down, but some won't. No matter what career you want to pursue, there are various approaches to getting a foot in the door. Shift your thinking and see what happens. You may have a mentor in your family … someone who is successful in a company that interests you. Most people don't think of the people "in their own backyards" as sources of information and assistance. When you don't shift your thinking in this direction, you may overlook an important resource.

You may find this approach unusual: For one year I did a "dual job." For almost six months on and off, I worked in a division in IBM that interested me. The "boss" wasn't hiring, and, when I worked in his department, he didn't consider me an employee, but he noticed me. One year later, he offered me a position, and I took it!

> **Story:** A young lady once asked me what I do if I'm feeling "down" or blue. She was surprised when I told her I sing. I like to sing the song "The Impossible Dream." The song is about a quest, reaching an ultimate goal. Your ultimate goal can be as basic as saying, "I appreciate you," to someone.

This young lady and I were also discussing Sigmund Freud who said, "Thought is action in rehearsal." (Freud was an Austrian neurologist, 1856–1939.) You might notice that many fine thinkers come to the same conclusions. But the reason I share this with you now is that it started me thinking that lots of people—such as Freud and Einstein and Edison and Jefferson—were project managers.

Are you a project manager? I believe I am. Project management requires disciplined planning, organizing ideas and work, and allocating resources so the end result is just what you want … the achievement of a specific goal. In the final analysis, the project manager does things to benefit others. And that's as basic as it gets.

Do it once and you can do it again! You may only have to shift your thinking a little to rise to a new occasion.

Story: Former secretary of state and retired four-star general Colin Powell was interviewed for an article that appeared in *Fortune* magazine (July 6, 2009). He told the story of a young officer who asked an older general for advice on how to become a general. "Son, you've got to work like a dog. You've got to have moral and physical courage. There may be days you're tired but you must never show fatigue. You'll be afraid, but you can never show fear. You must always be the leader." When the young officer asked if that was how the general got to the top, here's what Powell responded: "That's how you become a first lieutenant and then you keep doing it over and over."

I submit to you that, each step of the way, that first lieutenant will have a whole lot of *shift thinking* going on. He can't move forward if he's stuck in the same old mold.

Story: Dr. Ben Carson was awarded the Presidential Medal of Freedom, the highest civilian honor. President George W. Bush made the presentation on June 19, 2008. Yet Ben Carson was born into a broken family living in inner-city Detroit. In school, he was considered one of the dumbest kids.

I could write about Dr. Carson in each and every chapter of this book. Clearly, he has done "everything else"! To go from a life of destitution and underachievement to becoming a life-saving hero for thousands of people is quite a journey, and, happily, Dr. Carson is not finished yet. No doubt, he shifted thinking many, manytimes. His mother Sonya had a third-grade education, but she guided and encouraged her son. He graduated from high school with honors and entered Yale University. He earned a degree in psychology, but decided to go to medical school. He became a neurosurgeon. I speak of Dr. Carson often to my students, to seminar attendees, and to anyone who thinks he or she has it tough and finds the odds too challenging. *Shift your thinking!* You may want to read his books, *Gifted Hands: The Ben Carson Story* and *Think Big: Unleashing Your Potential for Excellence* (both with Cecil Murphy); and *The Big Picture* (with Gregg Lewis). He's a gifted speaker too … you can listen to him on YouTube.

Story: A young man set himself a goal—to walk onto the football field at University of Central Florida with the team. When he accomplished this feat, however, he was ready to walk away. I mentioned to him that, since the entire spring practice was not over, he hadn't completed the cycle. He had to *shift thinking* … to "turn" so that he could better glimpse the possibilities. He was about to quit in the middle, and he didn't recognize it.

We met on a flight from Orlando to West Palm Beach. I had the aisle seat, and the middle and window seats were already occupied when I arrived. I sat down and introduced myself to the person next to me as I always do. And that's when Chris and I met—officially. I had noticed him in the waiting area outside the gate. He was accompanying his grandmother, who was in a wheelchair, and, for some reason, I noticed how pleasantly he interacted with her (I didn't know then she was his grandmother). He obviously was trying to make her comfortable. I didn't know who he was and didn't have any idea I would soon be seated next to him on the flight. The flight, however, afforded us the opportunity to have a forty-five-minute discussion. It turned out we were even heading for the same destination.

"What brings you here?" I asked. He explained he was a student at the University of Central Florida.

"What are you studying?"

"Business, but the most exciting thing I've done there was walking onto the football field!"

"With all due respect," I said, "You're not a very big guy."

"No. I'm not."

"Chris, you're telling me that, out of 60,000 students, only fifteen walk on? I know UCF, and there are a lot of students who I know want to walk on."

"True. I'm number fifteen."

"Wow. That's pretty cool. What made you do that?"

"People told me I couldn't. I wanted to prove to myself that I could. I did, but now—it's over."

"What is the coach telling you?" I asked.

"He gave me some positive feedback, but I know I'm not going to make the team."

"You know this already?"

Chris confirmed he had no doubt he wasn't going to make the team.

I told Chris something about myself. I talked a little about the message I share with audiences. Then I asked him what he was currently doing for the team.

"Weight lifting."

"How long are you going to do this?"

"Three more weeks, but then it's over for me."

"You're only accomplishing half your goal."

"What do you mean?" he asked as he leaned forward in his seat.

"I want you to think about not leaving the team after you finish the weight lifting. Wait until the end of summer to make your decision. Then you can tell your friends and family that you completed the cycle. Your desire was to walk on; but you should extend your desire, if you will, to being able to finish what you said you were going to do, which is not only walking on but finishing the cycle. At the end of the cycle, you will have completed this practice ... you're not leaving halfway. Practice isn't over after weight lifting; it's over in June or over in July. Your plan should be like saying, *I am going to leave my job after two weeks' notice. I am not going to quit right now just because I found a new job. I'm going to do it the right way.* This behavior announces that you're a professional. After all, these people gave you a chance to walk on; these people took a chance on you. Your *higher self* will guide you as you decide you owe them the time and effort it takes to complete the cycle.

Story: When I was presenting at American Express, I mentioned to the team that most of us are catching the headwind in life—or the headwind in where we want to go. When it's not moving us forward, we can shift our position … just move around a little bit … and the tailwind catches us. Sometimes all you have to do is ask questions. You may have felt stuck before you did this "shifting." Go to your boss, your spouse, your neighbor and ask, "What can we do about this?" You can get to a new place.

You may be arguing with your boss, for example, and getting nowhere. "You're not giving me the right assignments!" If you shift a little and begin to help the boss understand … "Here's where we are in the sales cycle. That said; you can appreciate the challenges we're facing." Before you may have said, "You don't get it … I'm out of here. You keep giving me these assignments and you don't understand what I have to …"

Develop a *willing mind*, and you will find it easier to shift your thinking. The willing mind begets willing actions. Get up every morning with *a purpose* in mind. *I am willing to do this today.* I am willing to accept the fact that I can reach a higher self. Albert Einstein said that he did not have any special talents, he was just passionately curious. No talent is needed to be curious.

Lessons Learned

It's practically impossible to stand in front of audiences without having some of your thoughts pour out of your mouth in unique ways. Some of those words are worth saving so you can march them out another day ...

- We need to constantly be negotiating with our thoughts so we can win.

- What I desire is on its way ... it will arrive precisely on God's timetable, not mine. Everything that I am experiencing now is disguised as a problem, but I know that it's a blessing. What I desire is on its way and it's coming to me in amounts even greater than I can imagine. This is my vision, and I'll hold onto it in a state of gratitude no matter what.

- To develop a willing mind, start by shifting your thoughts.

Own It!

When you familiarize yourself with all that is in this book, it's likely you will almost never be down or blue. That's because you start the day happy ... you connect to the source—or higher power—and you ask the source to give you, for example, a person for whom you can "buy a bike." You're too busy sharing, connecting, and doing so many rewarding things that there's hardly time or reason to feel blue.

The world will be a better place, your company will be a better place, your relationships will be in a better place ... when you don't stop at, "Oh, I'm only a human being." Of course you're only human, but you're ... human! And you are hardwired to be a *learning* human. And you're hardwired to be a *contributing* human. And you're hardwired to be a *problem-solving* human. And you're hardwired to be a *leading* human. (Does this take talent? Absolutely *not!*)

Shifting Our Thinking

Your thinking has expanded ... exploded. It is no longer confined to following the path most people take or the path you once followed. Once you operate like this, you never go back to the beginning. You may go back to the middle, but never to the beginning. Remember what I said in chapter two? "The temptation to give up is at the highest level just when you are about to succeed."

A Very Short Quiz

1. Do you think of yourself as a victim? *Yes* or *No*? (For example, John is lucky. I'm not lucky.) Even when a person is incarcerated, he or she can still recognize everything needed to succeed is within. (I think of Nelson Mandela! Do you?)
2. People who write books exaggerate. *Yes* or *No*? That's like saying there are blue books in the library. All books in the library must be blue. Right?

If you said *yes* to the first question and *no* to the second, give yourself *5 points*! If you didn't … no points for you. If you earned 5 points, add them to the points you earned earlier. Remember the combined number.

Align your thoughts to your aspirations; the rest will follow.

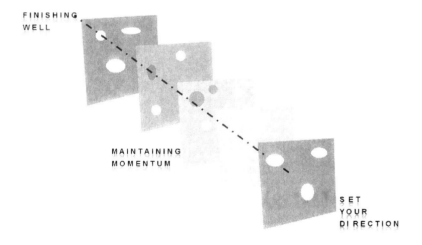

FINISHING
WELL

MAINTAINING
MOMENTUM

SET
YOUR
DIRECTION

CHAPTER FIVE

The Fifth Solution:
Buoyed by the Source

If you develop the absolute sense of certainty that powerful beliefs provide, then you can get yourself to accomplish virtually anything, including those things that other people are certain are impossible.

—Anthony Robbins
American author, motivational speaker

It is amazing what you can accomplish if you do not care who gets the credit.

—Harry S. Truman
Thirty-third president of the United States

I've learned … that we should be glad God doesn't give us everything we ask for.

—Andy Rooney
American television writer

I know that *nothing is impossible* when you have faith and take the steps necessary to achieve goals. Still, there's one thing I must add … *you can't succeed by yourself.* You may want to think of this phenomenon as the Universe being wired in such a way that you co-create with your source. Some readers see this chapter's title and automatically think about religion. God is their source. In order to succeed, they co-create with

God. Other readers see the chapter's title and broaden the meaning—they know how much they depend upon parents, siblings, a spouse, or a best friend for guidance and support and how the relationship is a two-way street: a little give, a little take. When I speak of "the source," I'm not exclusively referring to a deity. People seek advice, information, and comfort from various sources. Some people get what they need from their jobs. They depend upon people they "connect" with in the workplace. Some employees, for example, dedicate themselves to being the best they can be; even when they hold leadership positions, they know they're also students. They learn from customers, clients, employees. They depend upon mentors and take advantage of formal training opportunities.

Every one of the chapters in this book is peppered with stories that spotlight ordinary people doing out-of-the-ordinary things and obtaining outstanding results. I invite you now, as you explore chapter five, to:

- Read the stories.
- Mimic, copy, *steal* ideas and actions you can use!
- Use what you can now.
- Come back again, anytime, to read and review.

Don't hesitate to ask your source(s) for help. Don't be afraid to ask, "How will I figure this out?" The minute you speak up, your thought processor starts to kick in, and people and events start coming your way to help you.

By the way, when I was teaching the evening class entitled Foundation of Success at the college, somebody said to me, "I've got to get my thought processor working … to align with what I want." I was so excited because he was using the words he had learned so recently. Now, *he owns the strategy* and can use it forever. And then Arlie, who sits in the back corner of the room, said … "Mr. Hernandez, this *works*! I've had little things happen to me."

The students in this class have high school diplomas, and some college credits, but most of them are trying to get their lives back "into the middle." Some have had their past troubles with drugs or alcohol. Suffice it to say, many currently have or have had difficult issues in their lives. They are no different than anyone else when it comes to realizing that *You Don't Need Talent To Succeed, But Everything Else Counts!* I'm proud of them for being in school, and happy they're applying many of the solutions in this book and attending class.

Story: I use this Cherokee Indian tale about two wolves in classes because it makes the point of how to get from point A to point Z so well!

Here's the story: One evening, an old Cherokee man told his grandson about a battle that goes on inside all people. He said, "My son, the battle is between two 'wolves' inside us all. One is Evil. It is anger, envy, jealousy, sorrow, regret, greed, arrogance, self-pity, guilt, resentment, inferiority, lies, false pride, superiority, and ego. The other is Good. It is joy, peace, love, hope, serenity, humility, kindness, benevolence, empathy, generosity, truth, compassion, and faith."

The grandson thought about it for a minute and then asked his grandfather: "Which wolf wins?" The grandfather replied, "The one you feed."

Story: Some people disconnect from their source and allow their egos to take over. You probably won't be surprised to discover that while *ego* means *I* (i.e., me, myself, and I) and is synonymous with self-importance, it can also stand for *edging god out.*

From an early age, a young man, who is a West Palm Beach neighbor of mine, has won awards for his cooking and baking abilities. Everyone thought he was going to be the next Escoffier! As he got into his late teens, he was fond of telling people how terrific he was. "I'm the greatest chef on the planet," he boasted to his classmates. No one could tell him anything. They enjoyed the food and elaborate desserts he prepared, but since the repast came complete with lengthy soliloquies about his great talent, eventually people would eat and run—if they came to eat at all.

If it were possible, I would give him a copy of *Talent Is Overrated: What Really Separates World-Class*

43

Performers from Everybody Else by Geoff Colvin. Colvin claims, "Contrary to popular belief, what makes certain people great is not inborn talent. Rather, it is something called 'deliberate practice.'" This, you may recognize, is similar to my "everything else." Our young chef would benefit by "opening up" to others ... demonstrating that he cares about them ... engaging in some give-and-take. He should be seeking advice and direction from mentors instead of acting like a know-it-all. If he stays on the "I'm better than you are" path, he will never attain the greatness of an Escoffier, Emeril Lagasse, Mario Batali, Julia Child, or many others in his field. Obviously they excelled at "everything else." They had mentors, managers, publishers, teachers, spouses, and friends who supported them and helped to keep them on track. They likely gave as good as they got.

Failing to the Middle

Failure is in your own head! Failure is fear ... once you turn fear into courage or curiosity, you're free again. (Fear = false evidence appearing real.) Courage is inside of you ... but there are times you have to prime the pump!

Most people don't know how to "fail to the middle." They always want to start at the beginning. The beginning is far behind them. Why waste time going back so far? *I didn't accomplish X! Why didn't I get this promotion? Why did I break off with my girlfriend?*

When everything looks bleak, you may feel as though you're falling into a deep, dark hole. My definition for failing to the middle is never even getting close to the bottom of that hole. You stop partway down ... suspended by what you know. You ask, "What resources do I have? Who can I go to? What can I do about this?" Why waste knowledge you have acquired by slipping too far back in time? By now, you have more life experience upon which to depend, and there's no point in going "back there."

Be aware, however, that the tendency to stop using your thought processor is high when strong emotions take over.

The reason you failed (assuming you did fail) at the beginning is that you didn't identify your attributes—your thought processor and higher self—and never truly connected to them. Now you know you can ask for help. Sometimes, when you hear yourself explain what happened aloud, you actually "hear" something new … you acknowledge an inappropriate action or a hasty move and you know how to proceed.

When in doubt, connect to the source. The source will get your thought processor back where it has to be.

There's a book entitled *Remembering the Future: The Path to Recovering Intuition* by Colette Baron-Reid. It is listed in the suggested reading portion of this book. I mention it now because it tells of "the voice of an inner teacher-guardian that is our link to the unseen world of Soul. Its purpose is to guide and protect us." I gained great insights from this book, and that's why I mention it now.

T-Shaped Thoughts

It's useful to be a T-shaped thinker … someone who knows a great deal about many things … but is able to explain the value to others. Someone who isn't satisfied to simply follow the crowd unless the crowd is doing the best thing. The T-shaped thinker thinks for himself or herself. In order to come to satisfying conclusions, this individual "schools" himself or herself about many topics all the time. It's probably safe to say this person is a TSR (toilet-seat reader!). If you have never thought about it, it's a perfect place to spend time with a magazine article or two you didn't have time to read earlier. And no matter where you do your reading, make sure you read the entire article. Very often the most profound information shows up near the end of the piece.

The other night, Germaine, a student in my classroom, said to me, "You're a T-thinker and we're not." I was flattered by his comment even though he and his classmates really are T-thinkers. The fact that they're in the classroom tells us it's so. They took action to obtain knowledge so they can push out boundaries and get to know what they don't know and start to add value in many aspects of their lives.

> **Story:** When the O. J. Simpson trial was televised, many people watched it. The man was a well-known football player and actor, and people were curious

about him and the tragedy surrounding the murder of a young, beautiful mother. Nicole Brown Simpson had been divorced from O. J. Simpson for about two years at the time of her death. The criminal trial was probably the most publicized criminal trial in our country. I watched too, but I watched on two levels. I was especially interested in the lawyers and how they presented the case and themselves. I listened carefully to their words. DNA evidence was presented. In a cross-examination of the DNA expert that lasted eight full days, attorney Barry Scheck said something I have used for the last ten years. He said, "I'm not here to criticize the defense; I'm here to clarify what they're saying."

Wow ... *clarify* ... what a wonderful word.

At the next meeting I attended, I said something like this: "If I talk about the competitors, it's not to criticize, but to clarify things." This has been so valuable to me. If I had turned the channel away from the trial, I wouldn't have captured that expression. And I've had customers say to me, "You never badger or disparage your competition." And I say, "That's correct."

When this happens, you become a T-shaped thinker!

Think of the circumstances when you're debating (or discussing) something with your spouse or boss. "Excuse me, I just want to make sure I understand ... I want to clarify some things." Suddenly the exchange proceeds on a higher plane. And you can tie this in to parenting, coaching ... whatever. If you become a T-shaped thinker, you'll find that you grow much faster.

Story: Here's another look at T-shaped thinkers. A successful businessman owned five fine restaurants. He visited them often to observe everything! He noticed that no one ever picked up stray papers on the floors or cleaned the glass on the entryway doors. So, he did it himself. But he didn't understand what the employees could be thinking. They earned a very good living working in his restaurants, yet they didn't acknowledge the idea: "If I pick up that paper, I'm going to improve business. The customers will see a cleaner place, and the owner will appreciate my effort."

It's likely these employees are I-thinkers: "This is my job, it's what 'I' do, and 'I' don't have to do anything else." The T-shaped thinkers are I-thinkers who have evolved: "I'm going to go beyond the everyday, normal things that I do."

The T-shaped thinker starts to stretch a little more: "I can create better relationships. I can expand my career. My boss will have more confidence in me so I can tackle projects on my own. I can be responsible for new things since people trust me more."

When you become T-shaped, you open up incredible opportunities for yourself: "I'm going to provide more projects for you ... permit you to do challenging things."

Some Thoughts from Dr. Wayne W. Dyer

Dr. Dyer is an American self-help advocate (born in 1940). He tells us that we're spiritual beings first—having a human experience. He is considered one of the finest self-help and spiritual authors, and I was grateful to be exposed to his books and teachings early in my adult life. You'll find a great book listed in the suggested reading portion at the end of this book: *Excuses Begone!: How to Change Lifelong, Self-Defeating Thinking Habits*.

Some key points from the book that I thought I would share with you:

- When you believe you live in a friendly universe, then you believe that the universe—or God, soul, spirit, the Source, or whatever you want to call it—is something that is going to support you rather than work against you.

- There is a universal intelligence that we call God or Soul or Spirit or Conscious and it is everywhere and in all things.

The Source has not given you any tasks that you have no ability to perform. I remind you that you were born with the abilities needed for success. "He has filled them with skill ..." (Exodus 35:35 New King James Version).

I believe that God looked at your entire life, determined your path, and gave you the abilities you'll need to reach your goals.

Think about it: before going on a trip, you assess what you need and pack accordingly. Rainy weather anticipated? Pack a raincoat and umbrella. Invited to speak at a meeting? Bring your presentation. Going cross-country to see family members? Assume you will need patience.

Max Lucado (Christian author, born 1955) writes, "God promises a lamp unto our feet, not a crystal ball into the future." God packed you *on purpose* with the abilities required for the journey.

Lessons Learned

- If you "google" *Google* you get 2.1 B hits; if you "google" *God*, you get a million hits. Does this sound like a shift is happening before us? Just be aware of these numbers and how important the Source is in our lives.

- Sun, moon, wind are there even if you don't see them all the time; believing before you can see is where it all starts. Using our thoughts to generate this belief system is very powerful.

- It's worth repeating this one. What I desire is on the way ... it will arrive precisely on God's timetable, not mine. Negative things I am experiencing now may be disguised as problems, but I know they are blessings. What I desire is on its way and coming to me in amounts even greater than I can imagine. This is my vision, and I'll hold onto it in a state of gratitude no matter what happens.

CHAPTER SIX

———————— ✿ ————————

The Sixth Solution:
Number One and Number Two—Do Not Disturb

Love and success, always in that order. It's that simple and that difficult.

—Fred Rogers
American educator, minister, children's television host
quote is from *Life's Journeys According to Mister Rogers:
Things to Remember Along the Way*

Whenever two people meet, there are really six people present. There is each man as he sees himself, each man as the other person sees him, and each man as he really is.

—William James
American philosopher and psychologist

The energy you need to create what you want is in your thoughts.

— Ralph Waldo Emerson
American essayist, philosopher, and poet

One comes before two. It's a simple arrangement. Yet some people don't recognize it. Entire books on how to build strong marriages and strong relationships are devoted to this topic. It's not complicated … just decide who or what (for example, your spouse or your career) is number one, and who or what is number two. Other priorities (for example, earn a graduate degree, travel to foreign destinations) come and go and flip and shift—but don't attempt to do this with one and two unless you're prepared to face the consequences. And, as author Bruce Barton wrote, "Sometimes when I consider what tremendous consequences come from little things, I am tempted to think there are no little things." (Barton was an American author and advertising executive,1886–1967.)

Every one of the chapters in this book is peppered with stories that spotlight ordinary people doing out-of-the-ordinary things and obtaining outstanding results. I invite you now, as you explore chapter six, to:

- Read the stories.
- Mimic, copy, *steal* ideas and actions you can use!
- Use what you can now.
- Come back again, anytime, to read and review.

The spouse or friend who frequently calls with excuses for staying late at the office is really saying, "You're not number one!" The person on the receiving end feels wounded. Nothing good can come from this.

More people think of *themselves* as number one because their ego tells them this is true. They start each day as though they are the sun and everything revolves around them. The fact is, everybody matters. Everybody counts. This is true in your family environment and in your business environment. It applies no matter where you are or what you're doing. Sometimes a spouse, a son, a daughter, a parent is number one and you take the number two role. We see these actions in all walks of life, Hollywood, politics, business, sports, etc.... The most recent is Tiger Woods, where I believe he confused his number one and number two. And we all know the rest of the story.

Are there other priorities in your world besides one and two? Absolutely! But, if you keep number one and number two front and center when you make decisions, you'll stay on course. You'll give other priorities consideration, but they will not take the place of number one or number two, and that's all there is to it.

Making Plans in a Vacuum

You make a decision: *I'll travel more for the company this year. My wife and kids will benefit from my business success.*

But … what if? What if your spouse is counting on you to be home after normal work hours? Perhaps there's a project he or she wants to undertake, like continuing education. Or maybe your spouse simply values time spent with you and doesn't relish the prospect of handling everything at home while you're on the road for long periods of time.

What if your kids are counting on you to spend time with them? Maybe your son's team needs a coach, or he needs to improve his pitching technique and he's counting on you for help. Maybe your daughter expects you to help her with her science fair projects, or she'll soon have her learner's permit and always "knew" you would teach her how to drive.

When priorities are ignored or skewed, it's not possible to make decisions that achieve desired results.

Story: When I was a young husband and father, I was on a business trip in England. After work each day, I had plenty of time to think about many things. During my two weeks away from home, I realized I had made my career number one. My family had become number two. How had this happened? It wasn't acceptable.

So, to comfort myself, I scrutinized the situation. I decided to give *everything* a number one position … but I found it almost impossible to think about it! I tried to apply 1.1 and 1.2 and 1.3. Is my job 1.2? When I started to whittle away at my family's place in my life, I had to ask myself, *Are they really number one?* I decided my career was important, but not as important as my family. Paula and Brian and Jessica are my number one—without exception. Attending Brian's baseball games may get a 1.1 spot while Jessica's driving lesson gets a 1.2 spot, but that's only because the baseball game has a fixed time and we can be more flexible about a driving lesson. The only thing in my number one—do not disturb—spot is Paula and our family.

I telephoned my wife and told her I had "flipped" priorities almost without notice. I assured her that she was number one and I was going to make changes.

Of course, there were some consequences. I turned down some assignments, and my career paused for two to three years. Don't get me wrong—I still worked hard so my family could have a comfortable home and we could save for our children's college educations. But I put Paula and our children, Brian and Jessica, into a very easy-to-see place in my life. I visualized them standing under a big banner that proclaimed … We Come First!

When it comes to a career and shooting for a top position, a spouse may have to shift priorities. If you're aware of the dynamics—what is really happening—you'll work together to plan for the future, and you won't have false expectations.

According to some experts, "Elite athletes marry at about the same rate (73 percent) as everyone else, but their divorce rate is considerably higher." It's reported to be 57 percent. (Source: http://strengthplanet. com, accessed 12/2009.) Does this sad fact have something to do with ignoring the sanctity of the number one—do not disturb—and number two status? It certainly is food for thought!

In recent years, we have seen role models such as athletes, government officials, actors, big business executives, and others in positions of leadership flip number one and number two, and the consequences do pertain to all of us.

Story: As I write this book, Paula and I have been married for thirty-one years. The last fifteen years have been incredibly marvelous. For a long time, I wanted to be right all the time. When I reached my higher self, I realized that's a lot of hooey! No one is right all the time.

When Paula raises an issue I don't want to hear about, instead of mentally shutting her out—I pause and ask myself, *Is this a life-threatening issue?* Then I realize, *Probably not. Will it change my life dramatically? Probably not.* I can take the time to listen. It isn't going to take hours for her to "make her case," and, if I disagree, I can simply say ... "This is my opinion. We just disagree. I love you anyway."

These three sentences take the heat out of most situations. Say it to your manager, a co-worker ... almost anyone. How upset can a person be when you tell the person: "This is my opinion. I disagree with you. I still enjoy working with you ... having you as my manager"?

Sometimes, you feel angry and have to struggle to remain calm. Your wife is crying, or your co-worker is shouting. These people paint the world hopeless, and, for an instant, you don't see a ray of sunshine.

On one such occasion, I said to Paula, "It's very late. We're both tired. Let's go to bed and get some sleep." I didn't sleep much that night, and my head was filled with negative thoughts and how-could-she-do-this-to-me questions.

At the time, Paula and I hadn't discussed thought processor or higher self or any of these tools. She had revealed a problem she had kept to herself for many years. Suffice it to say, it was a problem that appeared to be practically insurmountable. Ultimately, it took a long time and considerable sacrifice to resolve the challenge, but I refused to go backwards. In earlier times, I would have stomped out of the house. The kids would hear shouting and doors slamming and they would want to hide. I shudder to think where we all would be today if that had been my response. By then I knew that the energy I needed to create what I wanted was in my thoughts. I realized that my thoughts were actions in rehearsal and I could turn myself around. I connected to my source. God is my source, and, when I realized I couldn't fix this myself, I asked, *Who can I go to? Who do I actually acknowledge?* I asked God, "How do I get through this?" Here's the answer:

- *Out* with the negative thoughts and hurtful questions.

- *In* with seeing a positive outcome and planning how to get to it.

The Man and the Little Fishes

At first, I was overwhelmed by what I perceived as the enormity of the situation in which my wife and I found ourselves. Then I reminded myself of this story: A man is standing on the shore and sees thousands of fish. They're flopping out of the water and onto the sand. He begins to toss fish back into the water, but can't keep up with the enormous numbers of flopping fish. Another man is walking by and says to the first man, "You're wasting your time. What you're doing doesn't matter." So, the first man picks up one little fish and says, "It matters to this one!"

I knew what I was doing mattered. I also knew it wasn't all about me.

I envisioned my "number one"—Paula and me—working together. I knew we would be a powerful team and we could make things happen. Up until then, Paula was not a very religious person. Since that time, Paula has become more acknowledging of the source. It became apparent to both of us that we could continue being part of the problem or we could become part of the solution.

As I write this chapter, I can tell you that this episode in our lives has come to a conclusion with a happy ending. It comes down to:

- **Never Compromising:**
  We've each got 8763 hours to use each year. That means that, even if I must devote 8000 hours to number one and number two, I'll make everything else fit into the 763 hours I have left! I never compromise number one and number two.

- **Accepting New Opportunities:**
  When new opportunities arise, they get assigned numbers three to ten (or fifteen!). If, for example, teaching a class gets a number three designation, time at the gym, which had held that spot, may get bumped for the duration. I have options, but number one and number two are sacrosanct.

CHAPTER SEVEN

The Seventh Solution: Welcome New Experiences (Reaching out ... Staying connected)

Life can only be understood backward, but it must be lived forward.

— Soren Kierkegaard
Danish philosopher and author

Learning never exhausts the mind.

— Leonardo da Vinci
Italian painter, sculptor, and scientist

The will to win ... the will to achieve ... goes dry without continuous reinforcement.

— Vince Lombardi
American football coach and revered leader

If you're a fine auto mechanic, you're always focused on *connecting* with auto mechanic information. You need to know what's new, what's old, what's recommended. Otherwise you may be an auto mechanic, but not a *fine* auto mechanic!

If you're a terrific teacher, you connect with information that relates to being a teacher. You need to know about new instruction methods, what's happening in other schools, all about parent-teacher relationships. Otherwise you may be a teacher, but not a *terrific* teacher!

As a motivational speaker with many years of experience in the corporate world, I stay aligned and connected to how to make better presentations; how to market my services; what others in the field are doing, saying, writing, earning; and what people say about my programs. I need to know if I'm reaching the people I can help and if I'm making a positive difference for them. At the end of the day, it's not about me; it's about the customer—the people I am serving.

In short, once you start investigating, learning about what you're doing or want to do, you're literally *connecting* to your desire, whatever it may be.

Continued learning keeps you competitive and sets you up for what's coming next. There's an old Buddhist proverb, "If we are facing in the right direction, all we have to do is keep on walking." Sir Winston Churchill said, "If you are going through hell, keep going." (Churchill was a British politician,1874–1965.)

Every one of the chapters in this book is peppered with stories that spotlight ordinary people doing out-of-the-ordinary things and obtaining outstanding results. I invite you now, as you explore chapter seven, to:

- Read the stories.
- Mimic, copy, *steal* ideas and actions you can use!
- Use what you can now.
- Come back again, anytime, to read and review.

One Foot in Front of the Other

Story: I was working for my MBA degree at Florida Atlantic University and *connected* with other students. I met Rob, and, although I didn't know it at the time, this young man owned a computer consulting company and was an accomplished businessman. When Rob learned I was planning to write a book and that I was a professional speaker, he told me, "I'm doing a success series at Florida Atlantic University and would like you to talk about your perspective on success."

As one thing led to another, this "connection" ultimately resulted in a recorded interview (heard by many people), a video that has been posted on the Internet (also seen by many people), an introduction to Rob's friend who works with underprivileged children … *a new connection!*

Rob and I started to talk about what we could do together to help more people, and I learned about a group of people who operate a speaker's bureau. I was directed to the person who operates the group, and she took the time to come and listen to me speak. Now we're talking about how to promote my book and how to get more speaking engagements, and she and her associates are assisting me to perfect my presentations.

All this from saying hello to Rob!

This connected to that; and that connected to the other; and, at one point, all the dots connected! Here I am *expanding* and stretching myself and getting all these opportunities.

Making a difference boosts my energy level. So, even when I'm busy, I find the time to stay connected. Staying connected promotes expansion, stretching, and fun! We've all heard the expression, "What goes around comes around." I agree.

Siddharta Gautama Buddha (founder of Buddhism, who lived roughly 500 years BCE) told his listeners, "Success will not bring you happiness, but happiness will bring you success." The minute you say, "I'm too busy" or, "I don't need to do this, I don't need to do that," the *source*, which is full of abundance, starts to separate from you. It is saying to you all the time, "I want you to connect, but you're not connecting with me." The source is the agent that connects you to anything else you want; your source may include books, experiences, and people. Sometimes all we need to do is reboot ourselves (Control-Alt-Delete for some)! Ask yourself if you are better than you used to be—a better parent, sibling, spouse, associate, employee? Trying to create a newer you is very difficult, but a better you is always inside of you.

How Do You Continue the Learning Process?

- Actively invite exciting and accomplished people into your life.

- Read some quotes. (See the last pages of this book for quotes.)

- Read books and articles and see movies about great achievers.

- Attend seminars that feature great achievers.

No matter how you happen to bear witness to their successes, great achievers can motivate you. They excite you and let you know that what you thought was impossible is possible! You will come to realize: If he or she can do it … maybe I can do it. Seek these people and get ready to have your temperature rise!

Speaking of which, there's a video entitled "212," which you should be able to access online (www.just212.com accessed 12/2009). Here's the opening message, "At 211 degrees, water is hot. At 212 degrees, it boils. And with boiling water, comes steam. And with steam, you can power a train."

The video makes a powerful point and demonstrates that it doesn't take much more than you're already doing to achieve a great deal more than you already have.

Introducing Les Brown

Les Brown is a motivational speaker and a best-selling author. That's like saying the sky is blue and the hour is late. It's descriptive, but the comment just sits on the page!

If I could shoot off rockets, I could better draw your attention to Mr. Les Brown and all that he has achieved, to say nothing of what he assists others to achieve.

"Leslie C. Brown was born on February 17, 1945 in an abandoned building on a floor in Liberty City, a low income section of Miami,

Florida, and adopted at six weeks of age by Mrs. Mamie Brown, a thirty-eight-year old single woman, cafeteria cook and domestic worker, who had very little education or financial means, but a very big heart and the desire to care for Les Brown and his twin brother, Wesley Brown." (This information appears on a Web site www.lesbrown.com, accessed 12/2009)

His list of achievements dazzles, especially since Les was, according to the Web site, mistakenly labeled "educably mentally retarded" and didn't receive much formal schooling. Today, Les is a …

- Hip-talking, morning DJ–*next stop* … broadcast manager
- Community activist–*next stop* … community leader
- Political commentator–*next stop* … three-term state senator in Ohio

Again, these words are descriptive, but it's just information that sits on the page. If you look and listen to one of Les Brown's presentations, you'll witness fireworks in motion! There's nothing quiet or matter-of-fact about Mr. Brown. Find him on a YouTube video, and you'll see what I mean.

I introduce him and his books to my students—but to look and listen is to be pushed out of your chair. His "mission" is to make people uncomfortable with what he calls their mediocrity. Don't hesitate to reach out and connect with him over and over and over again. And there are others who can inspire you.

Introducing the Phenomenon and More

Some things in life just can't be explained! In the movie *Phenomenon*, actor John Travolta plays the part of an ordinary man who suddenly has a dramatically increased capacity for wisdom and appears to work magic. Most viewers are probably surprised at the response of the man's friends and neighbors in the small town they all inhabit. A lesson this movie espouses is don't be afraid to be different. That message and the acknowledgment that some things in life just can't be explained can embolden us to aspire to new goals and to reach them. In the movie, the character has the ability to move objects with his hands, but without touching the objects. When he is asked how this works, he replies he doesn't know but that it's a partnership with one's thoughts, and anyone can do it if they allow it. To me, it's not so much about moving the objects but about using your thought processor to connect with your desires. The way he moved the objects is really about using thoughts to achieve goals—a better relationship, an advanced career, more time with your children, and so on. I'm convinced that our thoughts give us what we want and what we don't want! When you eclipse your desires with your thoughts, you become super human or, as I like to say, Super You.

Pizza Delivers

John Schnatter, founder of Papa John's pizza empire, might agree with this concept—some things can't be explained. He was planning to attend law school, and when I read about him in the September 28, 1990, issue of *Fortune*, I learned that he "bombed" the law school admission test (LSAT). He wanted to find something productive to do that would come easy to him. He asked, "God, just give me something I can do that I don't have to work three times harder than everybody else." The short article, "How I Got Started—Papa John's John Schnatter," gives the reader lots to think about. Schnatter reveals that one of the secrets of his success is to: Stay connected to customers. The company uses e-mail and Facebook to help achieve this goal. It's short and sweet, and you might agree it works: According to the *Fortune* article, Papa John's generated $2.0 billion in sales in 2008 … an impressive figure when you notice that Papa John's is third in sales just after Domino's and Pizza Hut.

You don't have to look too hard to find ordinary people doing out-of-the-ordinary things. I've listed some resources at the end of this book. Also, look for opportunities to attend workshops and seminars. Read books and watch videos in which dynamic people reach out to you. See if they have something special to offer you.

Now, I can't resist taking this opportunity to invite you to "connect" with me! At this time in my life, I'm able to almost fully commit my hours to helping others achieve success. With the publication of this book, I'm taking one big step in that direction. I hope that you may come to hear me speak or that you may decide to purchase a DVD that will eventually be available in the marketplace. (Does this sound like rehearsing victory? It is!) Come and connect with me. For me, this process is a way of life. Are you ready to do what it takes to polish your abilities—your "everything else"—and achieve the success you desire? You've come to chapter seven in this book of eight chapters. Logic suggests to me that, if you've come this far, your answer is yes!

It's Not All Roses

So far, this chapter spotlights the *up* times … the positive energy and the yes-I-can situations that result when you welcome new experiences. But some new experiences aren't about up times. When you first come upon them, they appear to be *downers!* Most of these experiences are valuable, too, albeit you may not think so when you're in the middle of them. I repeat what I mentioned in earlier chapters—the temptation to give up is at the highest level just when you are about to succeed.

> **Story**: There were times in my thirty-year career with IBM that I was unhappy. I didn't feel comfortable about some of the decisions that were made by me or for me. And there's a tendency to say … okay, I'm leaving. This is not what I want to do. I don't want to be part of an environment that doesn't do exactly what I want. In *real* life there are times when you're not going to be able to do exactly what you want—but, when you remain in that environment and adopt a positive attitude, you will make discoveries … you will learn and can be enriched by the experience.
>
> Someone asked me if she should set boundaries. She asked, "Should I stick around for a year to see if things change?" Boundaries, in my opinion, are imaginary. They're things we put into our heads. They're things that can distract us: *I'm only going to take it this far. Once I reach this threshold, then I'm going to make a decision.* But, sometimes, when you get to the threshold, nothing happens.
>
> Instead, find a new way to think about challenges. For example, suppose your boss asks you into his office and tells you he is disappointed in you.

- You may argue with him in an angry way: *You give me the tough assignments! You never give me any backup! No one can handle this client! She's impossible.*

- Or you find a new way to proceed … you communicate with purpose: *Okay, I understand where you're coming from. Let me explain to you why I made this decision.* In a moment you ask … *Do you see what I tried to do here?*

This is your thought processor at work! All the while you're listening, watching body language, learning from this argument. You're not busy feeding yourself statements like, *This guy has crossed the line!* You're connecting with your higher self, you're shifting your thinking, and it's possible you feel the comfort of the source washing over you.

A Clue—A Sign

I know I've reached a higher self when I'm not arguing about things I argued about ten years ago. I know when to let go, and I know when to continue the discussion. Notice how the word changes from *argument* to *discussion*?

Last time I checked the local bookstore, at least ten books spotlighted the value of being open to new experiences. No doubt, you'll examine some of those books since time and space do not permit me to explore this topic further here. But I couldn't close this chapter without mentioning that most new experiences have value. Resist the urge to turn and run if you feel agitated. Obtain more information and perform an attitude check. *What can I do to turn this into something productive?* By the way, some of those ten book titles are listed at the end of this book.

Young People

A few words about my son and daughter … they teach me so much! I've been on a baseball field with my son Brian (the San Diego Padre Baseball Organization and Vanderbilt University baseball) where there are 3–5,000 people screaming and I'm concentrating on my son hitting the ball. I don't hear anybody! I feel *connected* to him and I'm *helping* him. Other parents come up to me after the game and talk about the same kind of experience.

And it's a great pleasure to watch Jessica move from being a little girl to being a grown and responsible woman. She attended college classes this summer and curtailed her social life in order to give her studies the attention they warranted. Jessica likes people! She's got lots of friends, and I know it wasn't easy for her to say no to spending time with them. How can I not let go a little when she demonstrates this maturity? It's a new experience for me.

It's likely that neither Brian nor Jessica knows how much they "teach" me, but, in a thousand ways, they enrich my life. The "lessons" I learn spill over into interactions I have with customers, co-workers, friends, and relatives. Jessica and Brian help to make me a better person … help me reach for my higher self.

> *We make our living by what we Get, We make our Life by what we Give.*
>
> —Sir Winston Churchill
> England Prime Minister

Older People

I talk to my mother every day. She has many interests and reminds me of Cato, a wise man who lived in ancient Rome. Reportedly, at age eighty, Cato started to study the Greek language. When someone asked him why he was doing this at age eighty, he replied, "It's the youngest age I have left."

Will you and I welcome new experiences for as long as we live?

My answer is loud and clear … Absolutely!

Moving Right Along

When it comes to being "connected," I give something my complete energies, but, as soon as I move on to something else, I let the first "thing" go. I put my full attention … full energies … into what I'm "living." When I retire from IBM, I know exactly where I'm going. I see the slices of cheese ….

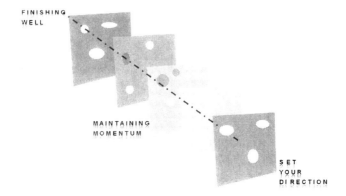

Life is a never-ending learning experience, and I learn best when I give my complete attention to the matter at hand.

Can you name one thing you learned today? American psychotherapist Virginia Satir (1916–1988) claimed, "We can learn something new anytime we believe we can."

Lessons Learned

- Have a conversation with your thoughts.

- Raise the bar … and leave it there.

- Pay attention: Read the tea leaves, see where the wind is blowing.

- Learn, contribute, solve, and lead. When you learn you have the opportunity to contribute. When you start contributing you can solve problems, and, when you solve problems, you become a leader. The promotions and opportunities start coming your way. The good news is that, when that happens, you start the cycle all over again—learn, contribute, solve, and lead.

- When you are not sure what you want next in your career, relationships, ventures, and more, I recommend you apply what I call the D-I-S-H method. Here's how it works: *D* stands for making your *decision. What do I want to pursue?*

What do I want next in my life? Once you decide, apply the *I*, which stands for *investigate*. Find out as much as possible about what you'll be doing next. If it's not what you really want, stop and go back to *D*. Once you have enough information and insight, you're ready to apply the *S*, which stands for *sharing* your ideas and thoughts ... sharing your decision with people who are able to provide you with more insight. At the same time, these people are learning about you and your aspirations. The *H* is a very important stage of the D-I-S-H method. It stands for *hold on*—hold on to your decision even when negative people tell you it won't work. When different opinions come your way, you have the *I* step—investigation—to lean on. You have made your decision with due diligence. (I've used D-I-S-H for the last twenty years, and it never fails me!)

- Be happy for other people's accomplishments.

- Watch a movie about a family's valiant struggle. These movies are easy to find on the Hallmark Channel. It's perfectly acceptable to shed a tear.

- When you are talking to people, show interest in them; look them in the eye and tell them you are interested.

- Use the word *potential* as often as possible. Tell your children, spouse, friends, and co-workers that you see their potential.

- Realize that it's not about you—it's about others. Let them know that everyone is special in some way.

- Don't forget to call the long-lost family member or friend and let that person know you have been thinking about him or her.

- Once in awhile, answer your phone even though you know you don't want to talk to the caller. The caller may be someone who admires you, and you will make his or her day.

- Buy someone a bike and get ready to experience the best feeling in the world!

CHAPTER EIGHT

The Eighth Solution:
Understanding *Have* vs. *Get*

My favorite quote is, "Let's start with what we can be thankful for, and get our mind into that vibration." Contemporary American mentor and coach Bob Proctor is the man responsible for these words. He continues, "And then watch the good that starts to come, because one thought leads to another thought."

I'm thankful I'm able to put what I've discovered into a book and share it with you. I have *lived* these discoveries … and know from the very core of my being good things can come into your life. It can happen to anyone!

The ability we need is already standard equipment in each and every one of us. So, if you're in a challenging place in your life right now, you have the ability to apply "everything else" and move to a better place.

John Wooden, the famous University of California at Los Angeles (UCLA) basketball coach (born 1910) once said, "Ability is a poor man's wealth." You can change *poor* in this quote to *short, tall, ugly, fat*, or any other adjective. It does not matter. You don't need talent to tackle challenges; you're armed with "everything else."

"The more you *share*, the more you're going to have. It's not the more you *get*, the more you're going to have." This lesson was taught to me by John Pandolfi. John was one of my managers many years ago when I was new to IBM.

Once the process begins, it never lets up. I don't wait for something to show up ... I just "do my thing" and know what I need and what I want will appear somewhere down the road as I move along.

Every one of the chapters in this book is peppered with stories that spotlight ordinary people doing out-of-the-ordinary things and obtaining outstanding results. I invite you now, as you explore chapter eight, to:

- Read the stories.

- Mimic, copy, *steal* ideas and actions you can use!

- Use what you can now.

- Come back again, anytime, to read and review.

Story: I needed money to develop this book and didn't realize how much money my IBM stocks were worth. I thought I had depleted the account some time ago when we purchased our house. When I—just by chance—took a look at a statement, there it was in black and white ... exactly the amount of money I needed for this book! As strange as this may seem, this happens to me more and more each day. Don't think about getting anything; just keep asking yourself, *What did I do today to benefit others?*

I have a willing mind. I get up every morning and think, *I am willing to do this [whatever's on my plate] today. I am willing to accept the fact that I can reach a higher self.* It begins with believing you can improve relationships, career opportunities—anything you wish to improve. Just work on shifting your thinking, and you will find it easier to perfect your willing mind.

Story: Alan was one of my co-workers at IBM who was ultimately laid off. Prior to his dismissal, Alan frequently asked for advice ... *How do I move on?* But that's all he did—ask. He didn't try anything new. He was complacent. He was filled with self-doubt and didn't realize that he had options. He was truly afraid of the unknown. (Forgive me please; this is the only place in this book where I linger, for a moment, on the *negative*.) No matter what I said to Alan, he would respond, "I can't do that. What if I make a mistake? What if I fail?" When he sensed my disappointment, he would say things like, "I'll wait until I use up all my vacation days." He kept inventing mental safety nets to keep from making a change.

I don't have any statistics available, but I'd guess that sixty-five people out of every one hundred are just like Alan! Yet the very same abundance that's waiting "out there" for you and for me is available to these people. To accomplish a great task, you must step out in faith and have complete confidence that your next step will soon become clear to you. Remember this wonderful advice: "Leap and the net will appear!" (John Burroughs, 1837–1921). Success is dependent on effort.

Gently Down the Stream

Dr. Wayne Dyer mentions the song "Row, Row, Row Your Boat" (gently down the stream). He speaks of rowing your boat—not another person's boat and not a boat someone tells you to row—but your boat. Then row gently down the stream—not up the stream because that uses too much of your energy. And there's more. You may be able to see Dr. Dyer discussing this song on the PBS specials he does from time to time.

The song goes on to tell us, "life is but a dream." Dyer mentions essayist and poet Henry David Thoreau (American essayist, 1817–1862), who wrote … "Our truest life is when we are in dreams awake."

Perhaps Alan will read my book. If he starts with this last chapter, I sincerely hope he will also take some time to read chapter four— Shifting Our Thinking. Change and grow and you can have what you desire. The more you share, the more you're going to have … the more you do for others, the more you're going to have. It begins with you. You are truly in charge. Start rowing! Row gently. Be merry as you go. You may not come upon the abundance the universe has to offer today or tomorrow, but eventually you'll be in the thick of it.

Your Purpose

Is it possible you already have some of the things you think you must get? When my daughter Jessica was a little girl, she was excited to be going to Disney World, but unhappy when she learned the family was going to stay at a Days Inn. She wanted to stay at one of the more elaborate hotels. No doubt she had heard about these hotels from friends. I asked her, "What is the purpose of going to Disney World? Is it to stay at a fancy, expensive hotel?" She immediately responded, "The purpose is to visit Disney World." Many years later, when it came to buying her first car, Jessica asked, "What purpose must this car serve? Transportation or impressing my friends or something else?"

It's good to ask this kind of question. The answers help to put wishes into perspective.

All Kinds of Giving and Getting

Story: A hairdresser who specialized in short hairstyles was pleased to have as a client a woman whose hair was just beginning to grow back after she had lost it as a result of cancer treatments. The client was thrilled to see the results, and, of course, she thanked the hairdresser for the service and paid her. The hairdresser got pleasure from seeing her client happy! She was thankful she had the skills and the opportunity to make a positive difference. Every time the hairdresser goes "the extra mile" for a client, she is connecting with her source, and the source "says," "I'm going to give you more. I am going to create for you because you're helping me create for everybody else." The source demonstrates that the more you provide, the more you shall draw to yourself.

Sometimes it takes months or years to get to the point that you just keep doing "good" and forget about "what's in it for me." You'll reach a point when it's a perfect moment. There's nothing that can get in the way. Your confidence reaches another level. It's "there" for everybody … no matter who you are or where you're from.

You may read hundreds of books and talk and listen to hundreds of people in order to gain understanding. Feel excited about all that lies ahead for you, but, when all is said and done, it's up to you to act.

Life leaps like a geyser for those who drill through the rock of inertia.

—Alexis Carrel
French Nobel Prize-winning surgeon

A Purposeful Challenge—And a last chance to increase your quiz scores!

Find a quote that makes you feel like you can do anything! Perhaps you have one in mind right now. Make some copies of it and place them where you're sure to see one in the morning and one in the evening. Do this for one week. By then you should have the quote memorized.

Accept this challenge and you earn *5 points*!

Repeat the process with an all-new challenge the following week and you earn *10 points!*

You're welcome to use any of the quotations you find in this book. As you may have noticed, I like inspirational quotations that get to the heart of the matter quickly and cause me to sit up and take notice!

You may decide to take on this purposeful challenge for the rest of your life. If you do, there's no telling how many points you'll earn, but, I assure you, the rewards will be great.

Figuring Up Your Quiz Score

Two quizzes appeared earlier in this book. Now is the time to take the points you earned and add them to any you earned by participating in the purposeful challenge in the previous section. Did you earn at least 25 points? If so, take a bow! If not, don't be concerned. You gained so much by reading this far. Still, the greatest reward is yours when you act on what you have discovered. So, if you didn't pay attention to quizzes and points and quotations, promise yourself you will *act* on what you have discovered.

Summary
Predicting Your Future

My intention in writing this book is to convince you that whatever you want to do with your life—even if you want to write a book like I just did—you have the *built-in* abilities to do it!

A Unique Design
Our bodies are designed so that wounds heal, nails grow, and a myriad of bodily functions ... well, function! You don't have to "tell" your body to heal a cut or bruise, and you don't tell your body to mature as you grow older—it's all part of the design. The very same thing applies to your abilities. You come complete with the abilities you need to enjoy success. Believe it! You didn't arrive on the planet with more or fewer abilities than the next person. You have what you need! *Use* your abilities. Allow them to shine. Work toward achieving goals content in the knowledge they are attainable.

Success Is ...
Success may be defined as *advancing confidently toward a worthy ideal*. And it follows that, whatever that ideal is, you have the abilities to attain it. This book serves as an alert and a reminder: you already have what it takes to succeed. Eventually this *truth* will be as much a comfortable part of you as your smile or your handshake. Then you shall act with confidence to make dreams come true.

> *Believe in yourself! Have faith in your abilities! Without a humble but reasonable confidence in your own powers you cannot be successful or happy.*
>
> —Norman Vincent Peale
> American clergyman and author

When I finished writing this book and realized what I had accomplished, my past flashed before me! I thought about my parents who brought my brothers and me to this great country. I thought about getting married at age nineteen, and how Paula and I have been married for thirty-one years and have two terrific children. I thought about thirty years of navigating corporate life and moving up the proverbial ladder. I thought about earning my undergraduate and graduate degrees. I thought about my stint as a college instructor and appearances on stage as a presenter in a great many auditoriums in front of people with varied backgrounds. I'm convinced that I didn't need talent to get where I am now ... I needed and used "everything else"!

Our thoughts and desires are the starting point for all accomplishments—not a hope, not a wish, but a pulsating desire that transcends us. Moliere, a seventeenth-century French playwright and actor, who was considered one of the great masters of comedy in Western literature, said, "The best way to predict the future is to create it."

I can predict my future. I've had lots of practice.

As I share these realities with more and more people, good things come my way and continue to come my way in extraordinary abundance.

You can predict your future too. Apply what you discover on these pages, and the good things that come your way shall be extraordinarily abundant too.

Even on those occasions in my career when I was in competition against or collaborating with well-educated colleagues, I had an edge! I can tell you without hesitation that I was able to get noticed or lead a project simply because I had "everything else" going for me.

The Future

We all have the ability to give to others ... to share what we have. It doesn't take talent to do this. I give special thanks for this particular ability and know that my future will be filled with more of the same. I feel compelled to keep on giving.

The chapters in this book are written with your success in mind. It won't surprise you when I tell you that my second book is "on deck." By the time you look for my next book, your own future will be well underway. *Make it sing!*

Now go out there and unlock what is already yours!

Hectorisms and Best Practices
Self-Test, Awareness and Personal Impact

1. There is no need to prepare if you don't care.
   Have I done this in the past? Yes_____ No_____ if NO, why not? _____

   What is your plans to apply the Best practice? _____
   _____

   How will I apply this in my Life? _____
   _____

   How will this make a positive Impact to the people around me? _____

   How does my Daily routine change if I apply the following?
   _____

   If I am able to think this way, how will I measure my progress? _____

   How will you start to share this Best Practice with others, what is your plan?_____
   _____

2. Ready ... set ... *have a purpose* ... go!
   Have I done this in the past? Yes_____ No_____ if NO, why not? _____

   What is your plans to apply the Best practice? _____
   _____

   How will I apply this in my Life? _____
   _____

   How will this make a positive Impact to the people around me? _____

How does my Daily routine change if I apply the following?
_____

If I am able to think this way, how will I measure my progress? _____

*How will you start to share this Best Practice with others, what is your plan?*_____
_____

3. Not only read, but learn.
   Have I done this in the past? Yes_____ No_____ if NO, why not? _____

   What is your plans to apply the Best practice? _____

   How will I apply this in my Life? _____
   _____

   How will this make a positive Impact to the people around me? _____

   How does my Daily routine change if I apply the following?
   _____

   If I am able to think this way, how will I measure my progress? _____

   *How will you start to share this Best Practice with others, what is your plan?*_____
   _____

4. Look for breaks in your life even if they're not necessarily the exact things you want right now. The universe in its wisdom leads you, in spite of yourself, in the direction of what it already knew you really wanted.

Have I done this in the past? Yes_____ No_____ if NO, why not? _____

What is your plans to apply the Best practice? _____
_____

How will I apply this in my Life? _____
_____

How will this make a positive Impact to the people around me? _____

How does my Daily routine change if I apply the following?
_____

If I am able to think this way, how will I measure my progress? _____

How will you start to share this Best Practice with others, what is your plan?_____
_____

5. Think, "How can I contribute?" That will lead to solving problems, and that will lead to opportunities.

   Have I done this in the past? Yes_____ No_____ if NO, why not? _____

   What is your plans to apply the Best practice? _____
   _____

   How will I apply this in my Life? _____
   _____

   How will this make a positive Impact to the people around me? _____

How does my Daily routine change if I apply the following?

_____

If I am able to think this way, how will I measure my progress? _____

*How will you start to share this Best Practice with others, what is your plan?*_____

_____

6. When uncertainty creeps in, know that the abilities to succeed are prepacked within you.

    Have I done this in the past? Yes_____ No_____ if NO, why not? _____

    What is your plans to apply the Best practice? _____

    _____

    How will I apply this in my Life? _____

    _____

    How will this make a positive Impact to the people around me? _____

    How does my Daily routine change if I apply the following?

    _____

    If I am able to think this way, how will I measure my progress? _____

    *How will you start to share this Best Practice with others, what is your plan?*_____

    _____

7. If you need to cry, just cry. That is just another ability we have.

Have I done this in the past? Yes_____ No_____ if NO, why not? _____

What is your plans to apply the Best practice? _____
_____

How will I apply this in my Life? _____
_____

How will this make a positive Impact to the people around me? _____

How does my Daily routine change if I apply the following?
_____

If I am able to think this way, how will I measure my progress? _____

How will you start to share this Best Practice with others, what is your plan?_____
_____

8. You don't have to win every argument. We can just disagree.

   Have I done this in the past? Yes_____ No_____ if NO, why not? _____

   What is your plans to apply the Best practice? _____
   _____

   How will I apply this in my Life? _____
   _____

   How will this make a positive Impact to the people around me? _____

How does my Daily routine change if I apply the following?

_____

If I am able to think this way, how will I measure my progress? _____

*How will you start to share this Best Practice with others, what is your plan?*_____

_____

9. From time to time, eat some Oreo cookies.
   Have I done this in the past? Yes_____ No_____ if NO, why not? _____

   What is your plans to apply the Best practice? _____

   _____

   How will I apply this in my Life? _____

   _____

   How will this make a positive Impact to the people around me? _____

   How does my Daily routine change if I apply the following?

   _____

   If I am able to think this way, how will I measure my progress? _____

   *How will you start to share this Best Practice with others, what is your plan?*_____

   _____

10. Call someone you need to make peace with; it will do wonders for your present challenges.
    Have I done this in the past? Yes_____ No_____ if NO, why not? _____

What is your plans to apply the Best practice? _____
_____

How will I apply this in my Life? _____
_____

How will this make a positive Impact to the people around me? _____

How does my Daily routine change if I apply the following?
_____

If I am able to think this way, how will I measure my progress? _____

*How will you start to share this Best Practice with others, what is your plan?*_____
_____

11. Don't compare your problems to those of others. You have no idea the path they've taken.
    Have I done this in the past? Yes_____ No_____ if NO, why not? _____

    What is your plans to apply the Best practice? _____
    _____

    How will I apply this in my Life? _____
    _____

    How will this make a positive Impact to the people around me? _____

    How does my Daily routine change if I apply the following?
    _____

If I am able to think this way, how will I measure my progress? _____

*How will you start to share this Best Practice with others, what is your plan?*_____

_____

12. If a relationship has to be a complete secret, get out of it.
    Have I done this in the past? Yes_____ No_____ if NO, why not? _____

    What is your plans to apply the Best practice? _____

    _____

    How will I apply this in my Life? _____

    _____

    How will this make a positive Impact to the people around me? _____

    How does my Daily routine change if I apply the following?

    _____

    If I am able to think this way, how will I measure my progress? _____

    *How will you start to share this Best Practice with others, what is your plan?*_____

    _____

13. Everything can be altered in the blink of an eye. Don't sweat it; God never blinks.
    Have I done this in the past? Yes_____ No_____ if NO, why not? _____

    What is your plans to apply the Best practice? _____

    _____

How will I apply this in my Life? _____

_____

How will this make a positive Impact to the people around me? _____

How does my Daily routine change if I apply the following?

_____

If I am able to think this way, how will I measure my progress? _____

*How will you start to share this Best Practice with others, what is your plan?*_____

_____

14. Take eight deep breaths. It does wonders to start your shift-thinking.

    Have I done this in the past? Yes_____ No_____ if NO, why not? _____

    What is your plans to apply the Best practice? _____

    _____

    How will I apply this in my Life? _____

    _____

    How will this make a positive Impact to the people around me? _____

    How does my Daily routine change if I apply the following?

    _____

    If I am able to think this way, how will I measure my progress? _____

    How will you start to share this Best Practice with others,

*what is your plan?*_____

_____

15. Go through your closet and get rid of 50 percent of what you have.

     Have I done this in the past? Yes_____ No_____ if NO, why not? _____

     What is your plans to apply the Best practice? _____

     _____

     How will I apply this in my Life? _____

     _____

     How will this make a positive Impact to the people around me? _____

     How does my Daily routine change if I apply the following?

     _____

     If I am able to think this way, how will I measure my progress? _____

     *How will you start to share this Best Practice with others, what is your plan?*_____

     _____

16. Whatever you have done in the past that has gotten you into trouble, assume it's not all your fault. But, from this point on, what gets you into trouble *is* your fault.

     Have I done this in the past? Yes_____ No_____ if NO, why not? _____

     What is your plans to apply the Best practice? _____

     _____

How will I apply this in my Life? _____

_____

How will this make a positive Impact to the people around me? _____

How does my Daily routine change if I apply the following?

_____

If I am able to think this way, how will I measure my progress? _____

*How will you start to share this Best Practice with others, what is your plan?*_____

_____

17. Buy coffee for the next person in line. Wow—what a feeling!
     Have I done this in the past? Yes_____ No_____ if NO, why not? _____

What is your plans to apply the Best practice? _____

_____

How will I apply this in my Life? _____

_____

How will this make a positive Impact to the people around me? _____

How does my Daily routine change if I apply the following?

_____

If I am able to think this way, how will I measure my progress? _____

How will you start to share this Best Practice with others,

*what is your plan?*_____

_____

18. All brains are the same—you have the same abilities as anyone else.

Have I done this in the past? Yes_____ No_____ if NO, why not? _____

What is your plans to apply the Best practice? _____

_____

How will I apply this in my Life? _____

_____

How will this make a positive Impact to the people around me? _____

How does my Daily routine change if I apply the following?

_____

If I am able to think this way, how will I measure my progress? _____

*How will you start to share this Best Practice with others, what is your plan?*_____

_____

19. Your thoughts are the shadows of your desires.

Have I done this in the past? Yes_____ No_____ if NO, why not? _____

What is your plans to apply the Best practice? _____

_____

How will I apply this in my Life? _____

_____

How will this make a positive Impact to the people around me? _____

How does my Daily routine change if I apply the following?
_____

If I am able to think this way, how will I measure my progress? _____

*How will you start to share this Best Practice with others, what is your plan?*_____
_____

20. Everyone and everything counts, even frogs.
    Have I done this in the past? Yes_____ No_____ if NO, why not? _____

    What is your plans to apply the Best practice? _____
    _____

    How will I apply this in my Life? _____
    _____

    How will this make a positive Impact to the people around me? _____

    How does my Daily routine change if I apply the following?
    _____

    If I am able to think this way, how will I measure my progress? _____

    *How will you start to share this Best Practice with others, what is your plan?*_____
    _____

21. Don't worry about what other people think of you. It is none of your business.

    Have I done this in the past? Yes_____ No_____ if NO, why not? _____

    What is your plans to apply the Best practice? _____
    _____

    How will I apply this in my Life? _____
    _____

    How will this make a positive Impact to the people around me? _____

    How does my Daily routine change if I apply the following?
    _____

    If I am able to think this way, how will I measure my progress? _____

    How will you start to share this Best Practice with others, what is your plan?_____
    _____

22. If you don't care, that is exactly what you'll get—random stuff.

    Have I done this in the past? Yes_____ No_____ if NO, why not? _____

    What is your plans to apply the Best practice? _____
    _____

    How will I apply this in my Life? _____
    _____

    How will this make a positive Impact to the people around me? _____

How does my Daily routine change if I apply the following?
_____

If I am able to think this way, how will I measure my progress? _____

*How will you start to share this Best Practice with others, what is your plan?*_____
_____

23. No matter how good or bad your situation is, it will change.
    Have I done this in the past? Yes_____ No_____ if NO, why not? _____

    What is your plans to apply the Best practice? _____
    _____

    How will I apply this in my Life? _____
    _____

    How will this make a positive Impact to the people around me? _____

    How does my Daily routine change if I apply the following?
    _____

    If I am able to think this way, how will I measure my progress? _____

    *How will you start to share this Best Practice with others, what is your plan?*_____
    _____

24. If you are having a good day, don't forget to tell your face to smile.
    Have I done this in the past? Yes_____ No_____ if NO, why not? _____

What is your plans to apply the Best practice? _____
_____

How will I apply this in my Life? _____
_____

How will this make a positive Impact to the people around me? _____

How does my Daily routine change if I apply the following?
_____

If I am able to think this way, how will I measure my progress? _____

*How will you start to share this Best Practice with others, what is your plan?*_____
_____

25. Your desires are waiting for you; they are not moving ... waiting for you to take action.
    Have I done this in the past? Yes_____ No_____ if NO, why not? _____

    What is your plans to apply the Best practice? _____
    _____

    How will I apply this in my Life? _____
    _____

    How will this make a positive Impact to the people around me? _____

    How does my Daily routine change if I apply the following?
    _____

If I am able to think this way, how will I measure my progress? _____

*How will you start to share this Best Practice with others, what is your plan?*_____

_____

26. What really matters in the end is that you are fair.
    Have I done this in the past? Yes_____ No_____ if NO, why not? _____

    What is your plans to apply the Best practice? _____
    _____

    How will I apply this in my Life? _____
    _____

    How will this make a positive Impact to the people around me? _____

    How does my Daily routine change if I apply the following?
    _____

    If I am able to think this way, how will I measure my progress? _____

    *How will you start to share this Best Practice with others, what is your plan?*_____
    _____

27. If you are tired of running, walk.
    Have I done this in the past? Yes_____ No_____ if NO, why not? _____

    What is your plans to apply the Best practice? _____
    _____

How will I apply this in my Life? _____

_____

How will this make a positive Impact to the people around me? _____

How does my Daily routine change if I apply the following?

_____

If I am able to think this way, how will I measure my progress? _____

*How will you start to share this Best Practice with others, what is your plan?*_____

_____

28. All of the abilities you need for success are available to you. The rest is just around the corner.
    Have I done this in the past? Yes_____ No_____ if NO, why not? _____

    What is your plans to apply the Best practice? _____

    _____

    How will I apply this in my Life? _____

    _____

    How will this make a positive Impact to the people around me? _____

    How does my Daily routine change if I apply the following?

    _____

    If I am able to think this way, how will I measure my progress? _____

    How will you start to share this Best Practice with others,

*what is your plan?*_____

_____

29. Don't forget the positive.
    Have I done this in the past? Yes_____ No_____ if NO,
    why not? _____

    What is your plans to apply the Best practice? _____

    _____

    How will I apply this in my Life? _____

    _____

    How will this make a positive Impact to the people around
    me? _____

    How does my Daily routine change if I apply the following?

    _____

    If I am able to think this way, how will I measure my
    progress? _____

    How will you start to share this Best Practice with others,
    *what is your plan?*_____

    _____

30. Never knowingly disappoint anyone.
    Have I done this in the past? Yes_____ No_____ if NO,
    why not? _____

    What is your plans to apply the Best practice? _____

    _____

    How will I apply this in my Life? _____

    _____

How will this make a positive Impact to the people around me? _____

How does my Daily routine change if I apply the following?
_____

If I am able to think this way, how will I measure my progress? _____

*How will you start to share this Best Practice with others, what is your plan?*_____

_____

31. If you don't expect a great day, create one.
    Have I done this in the past? Yes_____ No_____ if NO, why not? _____

    What is your plans to apply the Best practice? _____
    _____

    How will I apply this in my Life? _____
    _____

    How will this make a positive Impact to the people around me? _____

    How does my Daily routine change if I apply the following?
    _____

    If I am able to think this way, how will I measure my progress? _____

    *How will you start to share this Best Practice with others, what is your plan?*_____

    _____

32. Your abilities are inside of you. Your success is just around the corner, and the opportunities are all around you.

Have I done this in the past? Yes_____ No_____ if NO, why not? _____

What is your plans to apply the Best practice? _____
_____

How will I apply this in my Life? _____
_____

How will this make a positive Impact to the people around me? _____

How does my Daily routine change if I apply the following?
_____

If I am able to think this way, how will I measure my progress? _____

How will you start to share this Best Practice with others, what is your plan?_____
_____

33. If you are not looking for a better future, you will never find it.

Have I done this in the past? Yes_____ No_____ if NO, why not? _____

What is your plans to apply the Best practice? _____
_____

How will I apply this in my Life? _____
_____

How will this make a positive Impact to the people around me? _____

How does my Daily routine change if I apply the following?

_____

If I am able to think this way, how will I measure my progress? _____

*How will you start to share this Best Practice with others, what is your plan?*_____

_____

34. In the highway of life, you are allowed to change lanes.
    Have I done this in the past? Yes_____ No_____ if NO, why not? _____

    What is your plans to apply the Best practice? _____

    _____

    How will I apply this in my Life? _____

    _____

    How will this make a positive Impact to the people around me? _____

    How does my Daily routine change if I apply the following?

    _____

    If I am able to think this way, how will I measure my progress? _____

    *How will you start to share this Best Practice with others, what is your plan?*_____

    _____

35. You may be able to skip a formal education, but you can't skip learning.
    Have I done this in the past? Yes_____ No_____ if NO, why not? _____

What is your plans to apply the Best practice? _____

_____

How will I apply this in my Life? _____

_____

How will this make a positive Impact to the people around me? _____

How does my Daily routine change if I apply the following?

_____

If I am able to think this way, how will I measure my progress? _____

*How will you start to share this Best Practice with others, what is your plan?*_____

_____

36. Having a positive attitude is like fuel for a good day. You can always refill at no charge.

    Have I done this in the past? Yes_____ No_____ if NO, why not? _____

    What is your plans to apply the Best practice? _____

    _____

    How will I apply this in my Life? _____

    _____

    How will this make a positive Impact to the people around me? _____

    How does my Daily routine change if I apply the following?

    _____

If I am able to think this way, how will I measure my progress? _____

*How will you start to share this Best Practice with others, what is your plan?*_____
_____

37. You can develop a "mental six-pack" by applying "everything else."
    Have I done this in the past? Yes_____ No_____ if NO, why not? _____

    What is your plans to apply the Best practice? _____
    _____

    How will I apply this in my Life? _____
    _____

    How will this make a positive Impact to the people around me? _____

    How does my Daily routine change if I apply the following?
    _____

    If I am able to think this way, how will I measure my progress? _____

    *How will you start to share this Best Practice with others, what is your plan?*_____
    _____

38. If you want something done right and on time, go to the busiest person you know.
    Have I done this in the past? Yes_____ No_____ if NO, why not? _____

What is your plans to apply the Best practice? _____

_____

How will I apply this in my Life? _____

_____

How will this make a positive Impact to the people around me? _____

How does my Daily routine change if I apply the following?

_____

If I am able to think this way, how will I measure my progress? _____

*How will you start to share this Best Practice with others, what is your plan?*_____

_____

39. Why not do more than you are asked to do, to make an investment in your future?

Have I done this in the past? Yes_____ No_____ if NO, why not? _____

What is your plans to apply the Best practice? _____

_____

How will I apply this in my Life? _____

_____

How will this make a positive Impact to the people around me? _____

How does my Daily routine change if I apply the following?

_____

If I am able to think this way, how will I measure my progress? _____

*How will you start to share this Best Practice with others, what is your plan?*_____

_____

40. Don't believe the negative; believe everything else.
    Have I done this in the past? Yes_____ No_____ if NO, why not? _____

    What is your plans to apply the Best practice? _____

    _____

    How will I apply this in my Life? _____

    _____

    How will this make a positive Impact to the people around me? _____

    How does my Daily routine change if I apply the following?

    _____

    If I am able to think this way, how will I measure my progress? _____

    *How will you start to share this Best Practice with others, what is your plan?*_____

    _____

41. You don't need talent to be great, because everybody has the ability to serve.
    Have I done this in the past? Yes_____ No_____ if NO, why not? _____

    What is your plans to apply the Best practice? _____

    _____

How will I apply this in my Life? _____

_____

How will this make a positive Impact to the people around me? _____

How does my Daily routine change if I apply the following?

_____

If I am able to think this way, how will I measure my progress? _____

*How will you start to share this Best Practice with others, what is your plan?*_____

_____

42. An accomplishment is the beginning of what you want next in your life.

Have I done this in the past? Yes_____ No_____ if NO, why not? _____

What is your plans to apply the Best practice? _____

_____

How will I apply this in my Life? _____

_____

How will this make a positive Impact to the people around me? _____

How does my Daily routine change if I apply the following?

_____

If I am able to think this way, how will I measure my progress? _____

How will you start to share this Best Practice with others,

*what is your plan?*_____

_____

43. Don't ever think you are good enough to let up.
    Have I done this in the past? Yes_____ No_____ if NO,
    why not? _____

    What is your plans to apply the Best practice? _____

    _____

    How will I apply this in my Life? _____

    _____

    How will this make a positive Impact to the people around
    me? _____

    How does my Daily routine change if I apply the following?

    _____

    If I am able to think this way, how will I measure my
    progress? _____

    How will you start to share this Best Practice with others,
    *what is your plan?*_____

    _____

44. At this moment the reason why you don't have what
    you want in your life could be as simple as you haven't
    passionately thought about it long enough.
    Have I done this in the past? Yes_____ No_____ if NO,
    why not? _____

    What is your plans to apply the Best practice? _____

    _____

    How will I apply this in my Life? _____

    _____

How will this make a positive Impact to the people around me? _____

How does my Daily routine change if I apply the following?

_____

If I am able to think this way, how will I measure my progress? _____

*How will you start to share this Best Practice with others, what is your plan?*_____

_____

45. Having consistent "purpose" can accelerate your success exponentially.

Have I done this in the past? Yes_____ No_____ if NO, why not? _____

What is your plans to apply the Best practice? _____

_____

How will I apply this in my Life? _____

_____

How will this make a positive Impact to the people around me? _____

How does my Daily routine change if I apply the following?

_____

If I am able to think this way, how will I measure my progress? _____

*How will you start to share this Best Practice with others, what is your plan?*_____

_____

46. All you have to do is open your mind to learning and the teachers will appear.

Have I done this in the past? Yes_____ No_____ if NO, why not? _____

What is your plans to apply the Best practice? _____
_____

How will I apply this in my Life? _____
_____

How will this make a positive Impact to the people around me? _____

How does my Daily routine change if I apply the following?
_____

If I am able to think this way, how will I measure my progress? _____

How will you start to share this Best Practice with others, what is your plan?_____
_____

A Special List of Eight

This book contains eight chapters. Each chapter starts with one or more quotations. It follows that there are at least eight quotations that are especially worthy of note. I invite you to read them again. They inspire. Use them as a point of reference until your adaptation of this approach to life is so complete … it is second nature … it is who you are and what you do.

In this section, I'll list all the "start-off quotations" from all the chapters so you can review them at a glance anytime you choose to do so.

Here's one that's all new … and quite appropriate for this section:

As a quotation collector, I collect wisdom, life, invisible beauty, souls alive in ink.

—Terri Guillemets
American quotation anthologist

Chapter One

The First Solution: Reaching Your Higher Self

What you spend years creating, others could destroy overnight. Create anyway. The good you do today will often be forgotten. Do good anyway.

Chapter Two

The Second Solution: Rehearsing Victory—Prepare, Practice, Prepare, Practice, and Just Go with the Flow

You can really have everything you want, if you go after it, but you will have to want it. The desire for success must be so strong within you that it is the very breath of your life / your first thought when you awaken in the morning, your last thought when you go to bed at night …

Concentrate all your thoughts on the great desire in your life. This concentration must be continuous, unceasing every minute; every hour; every day; every week.

— Charles E. Popplestone
Twentieth-century motivational author

Chapter Three

The Third Solution: Feeding Your Thought Processor

You are today where your thoughts have brought you; you will be tomorrow where your thoughts take you.

—James Allen
British philosopher and writer

There is nothing entirely within our power but our own thoughts.

—Rene Descartes
French philosopher

It's a funny thing about life; if you refuse to accept anything but the best, you very often get it.

—W. Somerset Maugham
English author

Change your thoughts and you change your world.

—Norman Vincent Peale
American clergyman and author

Chapter Four

The Fourth Solution: Shifting Your Thinking

[Success] is the result of some good fortune to allow you to be in the right place at the right time, along with a willingness to work hard and make sacrifices; combined with the intelligence to know how and when to make adjustments; but mostly the drive to persevere regardless of any obstacles.

—Cal Ripken, Jr.
American professional athlete

If you correct your mind, the rest of your life will fall into place.

—Lao-Tzu
Chinese philosopher (traditionally sixth century BCE)

Chapter Five

The Fifth Solution: Buoyed by the Source

If you develop the absolute sense of certainty that powerful beliefs provide, then you can get yourself to accomplish virtually anything, including those things that other people are certain are impossible.

—Anthony Robbins
American author, motivational speaker

It is amazing what you can accomplish if you do not care who gets the credit.

—Harry S. Truman
Thirty-third president of the United States

I've learned ... that we should be glad God doesn't give us everything we ask for.

—Andy Rooney
American television writer

Chapter Six

The Sixth Solution: Number One and Number Two—Do Not Disturb

Love and success, always in that order. It's that simple and that difficult.

—Fred Rogers
American educator, minister, children's television host
quote is from *Life's Journeys According to Mister Rogers: Things to Remember Along the Way*

Whenever two people meet, there are really six people present. There is each man as he sees himself, each man as the other person sees him, and each man as he really is.

—William James
American philosopher and psychologist

The energy you need to create what you want is in your thoughts.

— Ralph Waldo Emerson
American essayist, philosopher, and poet

Chapter Seven

The Seventh Solution: Welcome New Experiences (Reaching out ... Staying connected)

Life can only be understood backward, but it must be lived forward.

— Soren Kierkegaard
Danish philosopher and author

Learning never exhausts the mind.

— Leonardo da Vinci
Italian painter, sculptor, and scientist, among other disciplines

The will to win ... the will to achieve ... goes dry without continuous reinforcement.

— Vince Lombardi
American football coach and revered leader

Chapter Eight
The Eighth Solution: Understanding *Have* vs. *Get*

My favorite quote is, "Let's start with what we can be thankful for, and get our mind into that vibration." Contemporary American mentor and coach Bob Proctor is the man responsible for these words. He continues, "And then watch the good that starts to come, because one thought leads to another thought."

Use the white space that follows to record some of your favorite quotations ... choose the ones you'll want to review from time to time. Choose the ones that inspire!

Sharing My Favorite Quotes

Don't go around saying the world owes you a living. The world owes you nothing. It was here first.

—Mark Twain
American author and humorist

Your future depends on many things, but mostly on you. If you are lucky enough to have done well, then it is your responsibility to send the elevator back down.

—Kevin Spacey

A successful man is one who can lay a firm foundation with the bricks others have thrown at him.

—David Brinkley

Sometimes the situation is only a problem because it is looked at in a certain way. Looked at in another way, the right course of action may be so obvious that the problem no longer exists.

—Edward de Bono

Lord, grant that I may always desire more than I can accomplish.

—Michelangelo

Life is like riding a bike. It is impossible to maintain your balance while standing still.

—Linda Brakeall

Don't expect a great day; create one.

—Author Unknown

One of the secrets of success is to refuse to let temporary setbacks defeat us.

—Mary Kay

Happiness is contagious ... Be a carrier!
To be alive at all involves some risk.

—Harold MacMillan

I always try to turn my personal struggles into something helpful for others.

—Henri Nouwen

Personal responsibility begins with ME. That's why it is personal.

—John Miller

Optimism is the faith that leads to achievement. Nothing can be done without hope and confidence.

—Helen Keller

We either make ourselves miserable or we make ourselves strong. The amount of work is the same.

—Carlos Castaneda

If you can't feed a hundred people, just feed one.

—Mother Teresa

There is one quality that one must possess to win, and that is definiteness of purpose, the knowledge of what one wants and the burning desire to achieve it.

—Napoleon Hill

Take the first step in faith. You don't have to see the whole staircase, just take the first step.

—Dr. Martin Luther King, Jr.

The greatest discovery of my generation is that human beings can alter their lives by altering their attitudes of mind.

—William James

Any thought that is passed on to the subconscious often enough and convincingly enough is finally accepted.

—Robert Collier

You have to put in many, many, many tiny efforts that nobody sees or appreciates before you achieve anything worthwhile.

—Brian Tracy

It's easy to make a buck. It's a lot tougher to make a difference.

—Tom Brokaw

Your life today is a result of your thinking yesterday. Your life tomorrow will be determined by what you think today.

—John Maxwell

A big idea is simply a small idea all grown up!

—Richard Rodney

Great men are they who see that spiritual is stronger than any material force; that thoughts rule the world.

—Ralph Waldo Emerson

I've got a theory that if you give 100% all of the time, somehow things will work out in the end.

—Larry Bird

Success consists of going from failure to failure without loss of enthusiasm.

—Winston Churchill

The minute you settle for less than you deserve, you get even less than you settled for.

—Maureen Dowd

Never forget that when you feel far away from God, it is you who moved, not God.

—Michael Levine

Leader of one, leader of many; if you can't lead one, you can't lead any.

—Anonymous

You'll see it when you believe it.

—Wayne Dyer

It is a fine thing to have ability, but the ability to discover ability in others is the true test.

—Elbert Hubbard

Success seems to be connected with action. Successful people keep moving. They make mistakes, but they don't quit.

—Conrad Hilton

Fear is useless
Faith is necessary
Love is everything!

—Martin Sheen

All the adversity I've had in my life has strengthened me. You may not realize it when it happens, but a kick in the teeth may be the best thing in the world for you.

—Walt Disney

The difference between a successful person and others is not a lack of strength, not a lack of knowledge, but rather a lack of will.

—Vince Lombardi

We act as though comfort and luxury were the chief requirement of life, when all that we need to make us really happy is something to be enthusiastic about.

—Charles Kingsley

Whatever you're ready for is ready for you.

—Mark Victor Hansen

Always do right. This will gratify some people and astonish the rest.

—Mark Twain

The will to succeed is important, but what's more important is the will to prepare.

—Bobby Knight

If you have a positive attitude and constantly strive to give your best effort, eventually you will overcome your immediate problems and find you are ready for greater challenges.

—Pat Riley

With clear goals and qualified people in place, teams are positioned to benefit from the power of teamwork.

—Scott Beare and Michael McMillan

Opportunity is missed by most people because it is dressed in overalls and looks like work.

—Thomas Edison

There is often in people to whom "the worst" has happened an almost transcendent freedom, for they have faced "the worst" and survived it.

—Carol Pearson

Just because you are in the driver's seat doesn't mean you have to run people over. Always play fair.

—Randy Pausch's father

You cannot change your destination overnight, but you can change your direction overnight.

—Jim Rohn

The greatest glory in living lies not in never falling, but in rising every time we fall.

—Nelson Mandela

Recommended Reading

Here are some books and Web sites I like to recommend to anyone interested in improving life:

Books:

Excuses Begone!: How to Change Lifelong, Self-Defeating Thinking Habits
Dr. Wayne W. Dyer—Hay House Publishing

The Seven Spiritual Laws of Success: A Practical Guide to the Fulfillment of Your Dreams
Deepak Chopra—Amber-Allen Publishing

Gifted Hands: The Ben Carson Story
Ben Carson and Cecil Murphey—Zondervan Publishing

Think Big: Unleashing Your Potential for Excellence
Ben Carson and Cecil Murphey—Zondervan Publishing

The Big Picture
Ben Carson and Gregg Lewis—Zondervan Publishing

Who Moved My Cheese?: An Amazing Way to Deal with Change in Your Work and in Your Life
Dr. Spencer Johnson—G.P. Putnam's Sons Publishing

Don't Sweat the Small Stuff … and it's all small stuff
Dr. Richard Carlson, Ph.D.—MJF Books

Slaying the Dragon—The Journey from the Dungeon to the Ivory Tower
David J. Koch and Brandon D. Hunt—Imacaulae Media

Remembering the Future: The Path to Recovering Intuition
Colette Baron-Reid—Hay House

Talent Is Overrated: What Really Separates World-Class Performers from Everybody Else
Geoffrey Colvin—Penguin Group

On the Web:

CareerAndYourLife.com–Unlock your abilities with some simple techniques
http://www.careerandyourlife.com

Simple Truth, the gift of inspiration
http://www.simpletruths.com/movies.asp

Inspirational Flash Movies
http://www.inspiringthots.net/

Inspired Faith—Encouragement for the Soul
http://www.inspiredfaith.com/index.asp

Hay House—Radio for your Soul
http://www.hayhouseradio.com/nowplaying.php

Letters from Students

Mr. Hernandez has showed me that by using methods such as (S.M.A.R.T and L.E.A.D.) I can accomplish anything I put my mind to. He also taught me by changing the way I talk and by staying focused on my goals I can make a positive change in my life. In order for me to live happy and successful I must never change my number 1 and 2, and those are myself and my kids.

So in conclusion my biggest accomplishment is that I have more confidence in myself. I would like to take the time to thank you Mr. Hernandez for helping me find this new found confidence. I Honestly believe that with hard work and dedication I can be and do anything. Now The only thing I have to do

ENDING THIS ESSAY WITH A BIG THANK YOU NOTE TO YOU, YOU HAVE MADE ME REALY USE MY MIND IN A WAY THAT ALL THE COUNSELING THAT I HAVE BEEN PUT THROUGH, THE ONE THING THAT MADE IT WORTH IT TO ME IS HOW MUCH YOU PUT INTO YOUR LECTURES TO GET THROUGH TO PEOPLE AND YES IF I HAD TO DO IT ALL OVER AGAIN BELIEVE YOU ME I MYRON BLUE WILL. SO AGAIN THANK YOU MR. H. HERNANDEZ

Two months ago, when I started this course, I didn't have a lot knowledge about a lot of stuff. But now after 3 months I really learn a lot and I gained more and more knowledge and competence in my life. I didn't know how "Shift back" to the middle if things are not going well the way you're heading. I didn't know about my "thought processor". But now I can manage my life, process my thoughts and they help me to be a better person than yesterday. I learn how to achieve my goals, use the VCR3, Altmm. etc--- From all of this I can say I really learn a lot from Mr Hernandez

Since the first day I walked into the classroom after I listen to the instructor I said myself this class going to be one of my best class ever. If someone did not have a chance to be in a Philosophical class, this class gives you an opportunity to be in one. this class help you build your confidence. It let you know that you can be whatever you want to be. The Way the instructor put the class together is so great you don't even want to go home. I enjoy every second of this class and I feel even ready to face the world with when Because I am loaded with Confidence, knowlede and competence.

Ever since I have been becoming more open minded though my tollerance level has gotten a lot better too. I owe all my improvements to Mr. Hernallez the Foundations of success teacher cause he really opened my eyes and changed my life and gave me the courage and the coinfidence to continue changing my life.

I am writing this letter to thank
you for you presentation here at
Campo Alegre. Although I am not a camper,
I was still able to learn from your words.
You were able to give me a boost of
confidence in trying to succeed in my life.
I was also amazed at all the visuals you
brought in as well as the interesting facts
you shared. I appreciate you for taking
time out of your life to share knowledgable.

CPSIA information can be obtained at www.ICGtesting.com
Printed in the USA
BVOW08s2220041213

338240BV00001B/32/P